A Dicti

IT S

Terms
Versio

Written and Edited by:	Ivor Evans
	Ivor Macfarlane
Published by:	*it*SMF Ltd
	Webbs Court
	8 Holmes Road
	Earley
	Reading RG6 7BH
	United Kingdom

Tel: +44 (0)118 926 0888
Fax: +44 (0)118 926 3073
e-mail: service@itsmf.com

© Copyright *it*SMF, 2001
This version first published November 2001

Based on other copyright material with the permission of the copyright owners. The *it*SMF would like to thank the contributors to an extensive international quality review process for their comments.

ITIL® is a registered trademark of the Office of Government Commerce (OGC). © Crown copyright material reproduced with the kind permission of OGC and the Controller of Her Majesty's Stationery Office (HMSO).

ISBN 0-9524706-5-9

Introduction

Many of those involved in professional IT Service Management over the years have recognised the need for a single comprehensive dictionary of IT Service Management terms, acronyms and abbreviations. The world of IT abounds with 'special' words and letters and a good deal of these seem to have found their way into this specialist aspect of IT management.

The authors, who have suffered the lack of a comprehensive dictionary as long as some and far longer than most, therefore determined to set the matter straight and have produced this companion to the *it*SMF booklet on IT Service Management, itself a working companion to the IT Infrastructure Library, and the 10th anniversary of the founding of the *it*SMF seemed an appropriate year in which to publish a first edition.

The sources of inspiration for this book are too many and varied for them to be listed individually but especial thanks must go to OGC for the work contained within the IT Infrastructure Library itself, to the British Standards Institution for the IT Service Management Code of Practice, and to Webopedia for their excellent online technical dictionary and search engine for computer and Internet terminology.

The authors are quite certain that the work is incomplete. Apart from the usual problem of having to decide where to draw the line, publishing restrictions themselves dictated that choices had to be made. However, it is hoped that all the words and phrases commonly met in IT Service Management publications and examination papers (and used in that context) are included and that the explanations given are clear and helpful. Should this not be the case, the *it*SMF would be delighted to hear from any reader who believes the dictionary could be improved upon.

Standard English has been used throughout the publication. An international edition will be published if there is sufficient demand.

Ivor Evans
Ivor Macfarlane
August 2001

4

Absorbed Overhead

Overhead which, by means of absorption rates, is included in the costs of specific products or services. Under or over-absorbed overhead - the difference between overhead cost incurred and overhead cost absorbed: it may be split into its two constituent parts for control purposes.

Absorption Costing

An accounting practice whereby fixed and variable costs are allocated and apportioned to cost units and total overheads are absorbed according to activity level. The term may be applied where production costs only, or costs of all functions are so allotted.

Account Manager

An IT Manager whose primary function is to maintain a close relationship with individual business representatives in order to promote the services IT can offer, to ensure that IT is satisfying the business needs of the customer and to explore new services that IT might offer the customer. Organisationally, Account Management responsibilities are often separated from Service Level Management responsibilities when individual customers receive multiple services from IT which do not have a common owner, or when Service Level Management is perceived as a purely operational responsibility, without authority or responsibility for service development.

Accounting

The process of accounting fully for the way the IT organisation spends its money, particularly the ability to identify costs by service, Customer and activity.

Accounting Centre

A type of IT organisation that identifies the costs of providing service, and may do some budgeting. The focus is on measuring performance and conducting investment assessment.

Action Lists

A specific IT Service Continuity Management term referring to defined actions, allocated to recovery teams and individuals, within a phase of a plan. These are supported by reference data.

Affinity / KJ Diagram (Jiro Kawakita)
A special form of Brainstorming (cf.) used to gather large amounts of ideas, opinions or issues, group those items that are naturally related and identify for each grouping a single concept that ties the group together. A useful technique when chaos exists, the team is drowning in a large volume of ideas, breakthrough thinking is required or broad issues or themes must be identified. This is a creative rather than logical process that encourages true participation because everyone's ideas find their way into the exercise.

Agreed Service Time
The time during which a particular IT service is agreed to be fully available, ideally as defined in the Service Level Agreement. Different levels of service might apply within the agreed service time, for instance the Service Desk might not be available for all the hours that users can access their services.

Agreement
In IT Service Management (ITSM) terms, the use of the word 'agreement' rather than 'contract' signifies less the legal differences between the two and more a difference in approach and style. 'Agreement' is used exclusively for an understanding, normally written, between internal parties (though it may be appended to and therefore form part of an external contract). An agreement is likely to register an aspiration for a particular service level whereas a contract will usually record the minimum service level permissible. The wording in a contract must represent its legally binding nature but the wording of an ITSM agreement reflects much more the nature of the (aimed for) relationship between the parties involved. (cf. **Contract**).

Alert
A warning that a threshold has been reached or that a failure has occurred, or is likely to occur. Typically propagated by a system management tool.

Alert Phase
The first phase of a Business Continuity Plan in which initial emergency procedures and damage assessments are activated.

Allies
Persons or organisations joined together for a period of time for a particular purpose or mutual benefit.

Allocated Cost

A cost that can be directly identified with and assigned to a particular Customer, service, activity, etc. (cf. *Apportioned Cost*).

Analytical Modelling

A software or other service component modelling technique using tools based on mathematical models.

Application Service Provider

An organisation that hosts software applications on its own servers within its own facilities. Customers access the applications via private lines or the Internet. Also referred to as a Commercial Service Provider.

Application Sizing

The process of determining the service level, resource and cost implications of any new application or any major addition or enhancement to an existing application.

Apportioned Cost

A (overhead) cost that is shared by a number of Customers, services, etc. This cost must be shared on an equitable basis. (cf. *Allocated Cost*).

Assembly CI

A Configuration Item (CI) comprising other CIs. (cf. *Component CI*)

Asset

Literally a valuable person or thing that is 'owned', assets will often appear on a balance sheet as items to be set against an organisation's liabilities. In IT Service Continuity Management and in Security Audit and Management, an asset is thought of as an item against which threats and vulnerabilities are identified and calculated in order to carry out a risk assessment. In this sense, it is the asset's importance in underpinning services that matters rather than its cost.

Asset Management

A standard accountancy process concerned with maintaining details of assets above a certain value and their depreciation. Asset Management systems may include information on the values, current ownership and location of assets in an Asset Register but, unlike Configuration Management, will not record the relationships between assets. IT Organisations that do not have a fully fledged Configuration Management Database will probably still have one or more Asset Registers, describing, in part, the IT infrastructure.

Asset Register
See *Asset Management*.

Assurance
The IT Service Continuity Management processes by which an organisation can verify the accuracy and completeness of its Business Continuity Plans.

Asynchronous / Synchronous Transmission
Asynchronous in a telecommunications sense is the ability to transmit each character as a self-contained unit of information, without additional timing information. This method of transmitting data is sometimes called start/stop. Synchronous working involves the use of timing information during transmission, which is normally done in blocks. Synchronous transmission is usually more efficient than the asynchronous method.

Attribute
Descriptive characteristic of a Configuration Item (CI), such as a make/model number, version number, supplier, purchase contract number, release number, data format, role or relationship, held in the Configuration Management Database (CMDB).

Audit
A process of inspection, correction and verification. Apart from their obvious financial application, audits are used to check the economy, efficiency, effectiveness and equity of an activity or process and to confirm (or otherwise) that an activity is being carried out to a common standard or in accordance with recognised best practice. In this sense, audits will tend to recommend, rather than implement, corrective action. (cf. *Auditing for Compliance*).

Auditing for Compliance
Checking that a process is being carried out in the planned manner, i.e. in accordance with its agreed procedures.

Automatic Call Distribution
Use of computing and telephony resources to direct a call to the most appropriate call handler in the shortest possible time, attempting to ensure that the caller is satisfied, that incoming call queues are managed effectively and that the call handling resources are efficiently and effectively employed.

Availability

An umbrella term that includes reliability (including resilience), maintainability, serviceability, and security. A common definition of availability is 'the ability of a component or IT service (under combined aspects of its reliability, maintainability and security) to perform its required function at a stated instant or over a stated period of time'. Service availability is sometimes expressed as an availability percentage, i.e. the proportion of time that the service is actually available for use by the customers within the agreed service time:

(Agreed Service Time − Downtime) / Agreed Service Time * 100

However this definition of service availability is generally considered to be archaic and immeasurable to any party's real satisfaction in a modern IT environment. Current best practice suggests that availability should be expressed in business centric terms, focussing on the impact of unavailability on business processes.

Availability Management

A Service Management process that helps to define Customers' requirements for IT service availability, understanding the capabilities of the IT infrastructure to deliver those levels of availability, and takes action to improve availability. Although there is a strong technical element to this process it is important that the overriding concern is to understand availability (and particularly the impact of non-availability) in business terms.

Availability Management Database

A database used by Availability Management for information needed to support report generation, statistical analysis and availability forecasting.

Availability Plan

A long-term plan for the improvement of IT availability within an agreed cost.

Back-office / Back-end

The business processes and operational functions that occur internally or through the supply chain. These often include inventory management, purchasing and distribution, order processing and tracking and shipping and receiving.

Back-out Plan

A plan that documents all actions to be taken to restore the service if the associated Change or Release fails or partially fails. Back-out plans may provide for a full or partial reversal. In extreme circumstances they may simply call for the IT Service Continuity Plan to be invoked.

Balance Check

A calculation that checks whether all direct and indirect costs (the total costs of IT provision) have been assigned to customers or services.

Balanced Scorecard

An aid to organisational performance management. The balance should be found between four perspectives: Customers, Internal Processes, Learning and Growth and Financial.

Bandwidth

The amount of information that can be carried by a communications line within a given time - normally measured in bits per second.

Baseline

A snapshot of the state of a Configuration Item (CI) or set of CIs frozen at a point in time for a particular purpose. A baseline will often be recorded to ensure that the infrastructure can be restored to a trusted state should a Change fail or the CI need to be re-built. A baseline will also be established for the roll out of new CIs and for use in a disaster recovery situation.

Although a position, such as that described in a project plan, may be updated later, the baseline remains unchanged and available as a reference of the original state and as a comparison against the current position.

Baselining

Process by which the quality and cost effectiveness of a service is assessed, usually in advance of a change to the service. Baselining usually includes comparison of the service before and after the Change or analysis of trend information. The term Benchmarking is normally used if the comparison is made against other enterprises.

Batch Processing

Executing a series of non-interactive jobs in a given sequence. The term originated in the days when punched cards were the normal means of entering data into a computer, usually a mainframe. Each batch of cards represented a job. Batch jobs are often stored up during normal working hours and then executed during the evening or whenever the computer is less busy. Once a batch job begins, it continues until it is complete or until an error occurs. Batch processing implies that there is no interaction with the User while the program is being executed. The opposite of Batch Processing is Transaction or *Interactive Processing* (cf.).

Benchmarking

A form of comparison, usually between the activities of one organisation and those of one or more comparable external organisations. Also used to describe a form of simulation modelling where the entire operational environment is replicated or simulated.

Billing

The process of producing an invoice or a bill and recovering the funds from the customer.

Brainstorming

A Problem Management technique used to quickly generate, clarify and evaluate a sizeable list of ideas, Problems, issues, themes, etc. by documenting 'what we know' as a team, tapping the creative thinking of the team and getting everyone involved. The technique is particularly useful in identifying possible causes when constructing a *Cause/Effect Diagram* (cf.).

British Quality Foundation

Together with the European Foundation for Quality Management – the bodies that promote the Business Excellence Model, a formalised approach to Total Quality Management (best practice in processes) that can be applied both to the business and the delivery of IT.

British Standards Institution
The body responsible for creating and maintaining British Standards, including those for IT Service Management.

BS 15000
The British Standards Institution 'Specification for IT service management'.

BS 7799-1:2000
The British Standards Institution 'Code of practice for information security management'. Also referenced as ISO/IEC 17799:2000.

Budgeting
The process of forecasting and controlling expenditure. It consists of a periodic negotiation cycle to set budgets (usually annual) and the day-to-day monitoring and adjustment of current budgets based upon actual or predicted outturns.

Build
The final stage in producing a usable configuration. The process involves taking one or more input Configuration Items and processing (building) them to create one or more output Configuration Items e.g. software compile and load.

Build Environment
See *Live Build Environment, Test Build Environment.*

Business Activity Levels
The predicted or historic levels of business process activity that are to be or have been supported by the IT infrastructure. Measured in business terms (e.g. number of account holders).

Business Capacity Management
A Capacity Management activity responsible for ensuring that the future business requirements for IT services are considered, planned and implemented in a cost effective and timely fashion. Business Capacity Management has a strong relationship with Service Level Management.

Business Case
Information that describes the justification for setting up and continuing a project or procurement. It provides the reasons for the expenditure and is updated at key points during the project or procurement process.

Business Continuity Management

Anticipating Incidents which may affect critical business functions and processes and ensuring that the organisation is capable of responding to such Incidents in a planned and rehearsed manner.

Business Continuity Objective

The desired time within which business processes should be recovered, and the minimum staff, assets and services required within this time.

Business Continuity Plan

Documents describing the roles, responsibilities and actions necessary to resume business processes following a disruption. The Business Continuity Plan will provide a defining structure for and exert a major influence upon the development of IT continuity plans. Its scope both encompasses and exceeds IT Service Continuity Management and is normally a business responsibility.

Business Continuity Plan Framework

A template Business Continuity Plan (BCP), or set of plans, produced to allow the structure and proposed contents to be agreed before the detailed BCP is produced.

Business Continuity Planning

Planning for the resilience and recovery of all identified business processes and support activities.

Business Continuity Team

One of a number of groups of people with defined, agreed and documented roles within the business recovery process.

Business Function

A business unit within an organisation, e.g. a department, division, branch.

Business Impact Analysis

A formal analysis of the affect on the business if a specific set of IT services are not available. It will also identify the minimum set of services that an organisation will require to continue operating.

Business/IT Alignment

An approach to the delivery of IT services to the business that recognises the pre-eminence of business needs. BITA encompasses ways of organising, managing, controlling and measuring Information Systems (IS) resources so as to maximise added value to the business and includes:

- Business Assessment
  - Value chain analysis
  - Ascertain business goals
  - Define IT requirements
- IT Strategy development
  - Formulate IT principles
  - Define policies and standards
  - Determine IT capability
  - Define technical architecture
  - Define IT process model
  - Define IT organisational model
- Customer Relationship Management
  - Market IT services
  - Customer satisfaction review
  - Customer liaison
  - Strategic business reporting
  - Define customer support requirements
  - Identify new service needs.

Business Objectives

The measurable targets designed to help an organisation achieve its overall business strategy.

Business Operations

Activities and procedures carried out by the User community in performing the business role of an organisation. A Service Desk is concerned with supporting and dealing with the comments and requests arising from those business operations.

Business Process

A series of related business activities aimed at achieving one or more business objectives in a measurable manner. Typical business processes include receiving orders, marketing services, selling products, delivering services, distributing products, invoicing for services, accounting for money received. A business process will usually depend upon several business functions for support, e.g. IT, personnel, accommodation. A business process will rarely operate in isolation, i.e. other business processes will depend on it and it will depend on other processes. (cf. **Process**).

Business Recovery
See **Business Continuity.**

Business Relationship Manager
See **Account Manager.**

Business Representative
See **Customer.**

Business Service
A service that is clearly identifiable by business representatives and has a clear link to the business' value chain, interfacing closely with explicit business processes. Most business services will have an easily identifiable senior business representative, are composed of a number of specific applications and rely for their delivery upon the correct functioning of infrastructure services. Service Level Objectives and Service Level Agreements should be formulated at the Business Service Level. The provision of all logistic components underpinning the sale of consumer goods is a typical example of a business service.

To achieve a productive and healthy **Business/IT Alignment** (cf.) it is important that IT services are clearly linked to the individual business services they underpin and in a mature Service Management environment, the Customer's business services will be top-level Configuration Items (CIs).

Business Unit
A segment of the business entity which both receives revenues and causes and controls expenditure. Such revenues and expenditure are used to evaluate segmental performance.

Business Value Chain
A sequence of activities that creates a product or service in which each step of the sequence adds something that the customer values. IT's contribution to that value chain should be understood and valued. In cases where this proves difficult it is probable that the service has been defined at the wrong level.

Call Centre

A business/customer interface where the emphasis is on handling large call volumes of telephone-based transactions, perhaps for commodity telesales services, queries or complaints.

Call Type

Calls to a Service Desk may be of a number of types; end users reporting Incidents are one, Service Requests another. Compliments and complaints are further examples of call types. Calls to the Service Desk are considered to be operational events that require managing. Other events will occur and may also be brought to the attention of Service Desk staff, e.g. through the automatic detection of an operational event that needs to be recorded as an Incident.

Capability Maturity Model

Developed and maintained by the Software Engineering Institute (SEI), part of the Carnegie Mellon University in Pittsburgh, CMM provides an arrangement into five maturity levels for software development: initial, repeatable, defined, managed, and optimising. Each maturity level indicates process capability and contains a number of key processes directed at achieving goals and organised by common features, which address implementation and themselves contain key practices that describe activities or infrastructure. The CMM thus enables the software development organisation to consciously choose a certain target level of maturity, and then to work towards that level.

Capacity

The maximum power, performance, content or output of a system or component.

Capacity Management

The Service Management process tasked with defining the business's requirements for IT capacity, in both business and technical terms, and understanding and presenting the consequences of delivering those volumes of activities through the IT infrastructure at the right time and at optimal cost.

Capacity Management Database
The database(s) used by all activities in Capacity Management, which contains technical, business, financial, service and utilisation data.

Capacity Plan
An output of the Capacity Management process. The Capacity Plan predicts demand for IT services and outlines the resources needed to meet this. It will contain costed possible scenarios for IT services together with a recommended option.

Capacity Planning
The task of providing plans and reports to meet current and future business workloads.

Capital Cost
The cost of purchasing any major item that will be viewed and recorded as an asset of the organisation, e.g. a building, hardware or software. The initial value of the asset is depreciated over a period of time (which may represent the perceived useful life of the asset) and the depreciation is charged against more than one accounting period. Capital Costs are usually a fixed costs and may also be referred to as 'one-off costs'. It is also possible for the market value of the asset to increase over time.

Capital Investment Appraisal
The process of evaluating proposed investment in specific fixed assets and the benefits to be obtained from their acquisition. The techniques used in the evaluation can be summarised as non-discounting methods (i.e. simple pay-back), return on capital employed and discounted cash flow methods (i.e. yield, net present value and discounted pay-back). (cf. *Investment Appraisal*).

Capital Item
An item maintained on an organisation's asset register and depreciated over more than one accounting period.

Capitalisation
Many organisations choose to identify major expenditure as Capital, whether there is a substantial asset or not, in order to reduce the impact of such expenditure on the current financial year. This is referred to as 'Capitalisation'. The most common item for this to be applied to is software, whether developed in-house or purchased.

Categorisation
See *Incident Categorisation.*

Category
Classification of a group of Configuration Items e.g. hardware, Changes, Problems.

Cause / Effect Diagram (Fishbone / Ishikawa)
A technique used by Problem Management to organise and display the various theories about what may be the root cause of the Problem. It focuses attention on one specific Problem (having made sure that everyone agrees what the Problem is), encourages innovative thinking (but not solutions, only possible causes) and provides a graphic representation of relationships (if too many, Multivote!). (cf. *Multivoting*).

CCTA Risk Analysis & Management Method
CRAMM® is a tool for analysis and management of IT security risks, suitable for use by the IT Service Continuity and Availability Management processes. It provides an insight into the risks to which an organisation is exposed and its use is often considered an essential first step towards attaining ISO 17799, the international standard for information security management.

Central Computer and Telecommunications Agency
The CCTA was the UK Government Centre for Information Systems responsible for producing and maintaining ITIL. Now subsumed within the Office of Government Commerce (OGC).

Certification
The formal evaluation of an organisation's processes by an independent and accredited body against a defined standard and the issuing of a certificate indicating conformance.

Change
Any deliberate action that alters the form, fit or function of Configuration Items (CIs) - typically, an addition, modification, movement or deletion that impacts on the IT Infrastructure .

Change Advisory Board

An authoritative and representative group of people who are responsible for assessing, from both a business and a technical viewpoint, all high impact Requests for Change (RFCs). They advise Change Management on the priorities of RFCs and propose allocations of resources to implement those Changes. The Change Advisory Board (CAB) will be made up of Customer, User and IT representatives and may also include, depending upon the nature of the Changes being considered, 3rd party and other administrative business representatives. The CAB is chaired by the Change Manager.

Change Advisory Board / Emergency Committee

An emergency meeting of the CAB, usually with a reduced number of members, to consider urgent, high impact Changes. Its membership, which may change from occasion to occasion, therefore needs to represent the knowledge and authority required in these exceptional circumstances. In practice, members may make their decisions without a physical meeting.

Change Authority

In project management terms, a sub-group given the authority to approve change within the project and sometimes referred to as the Configuration Board. If there were service implications, the Change Authority would need to refer the proposed Change to the Change Manager.

Change Control

The procedures to ensure that all Changes are controlled, including the submission, recording, analysis, decision making, approval, implementation and post-implementation review of the Change.

Change History

Auditable information that records, for example, what was done, when it was done, by whom and why.

Change Log

A log of Requests for Change raised during a project, for example, showing information on each Change, its evaluation, what decisions have been made and its current status, e.g. raised, reviewed, approved, implemented, closed.

Change Management

The Service Management process responsible for controlling and managing requests to effect changes (RFCs) to the IT Infrastructure or any aspect of IT services to promote business benefit while minimising the risk of disruption to services. Change Management also controls and manages the implementation of those changes that are subsequently given approval.

Change Model

A standard way of dealing with Changes of a specific type or complexity; consisting of a pre-selected and sequenced set of activities and roles through which a Change will proceed in order to ensure the consistent implementation of similar types of Changes. Change models may be built for major (project based) or minor (desktop move) types of Changes. The aim of a Change model is to facilitate the accurate and timely assessment of Changes by the appropriate groups of people. It also allows the definition of workflows and responsibilities for the building and testing of Changes.

Change Record

A record containing details of which Configuration Items (CIs) are affected by an authorised Change (planned or implemented) and how. The Change Record is created from an accepted Request for Change (RFC).

Change Schedule

See *Forward Schedule of Change.*

Change Slot

A regular, agreed time when Changes can be introduced with minimum impact on services.

Charging

The process of establishing charges and raising bills/invoices for the recovery of costs from customers. Charges need to be seen as simple, understandable, fair and realistic.

Charging Policy

The strategic role of charging, the level and style of recovery and the way in which charging will be introduced and maintained.

Charging System

A set of inter-related policies, activities and tools that enable an IT service provider to recover its costs from Customers.

CI Type
Configuration Items (CIs) classified according to their common attributes or purpose. This is different from a baseline in that it is a high level classification and does not specify a configuration.

Classification
The process of formally grouping Configuration Items (CIs) by type, e.g. hardware, software, accommodation, people, documents, business processes, external services.

The process of formally identifying Changes by type, e.g. project scope change request, corrective change request, innovative function change request, technical infrastructure change request.

The process of formally identifying Incidents, Problems and Known Errors by origin, symptoms and cause. The classification data strings, which are likely to include information on business impact and urgency, are essentially part of the Incident Record for automated matching of new Incidents against the Problems/Known Errors database. A distinction is normally made between the initial, or opening, classification (the symptoms) and the final, or closing, classification (the cause).

Clerical Backup
In case of contingency, delivering some part of the required services without the IT infrastructure. Nowadays, as well as some manual processes, this is likely to be via standalone PCs and commercial office systems software.

Client
The client part of a **Client-Server Architecture** (cf.). Typically, a client is an application that runs on a Personal Computer or Workstation and relies on a Server to perform some operations. For example, an e-mail client is an application that enables you to send and receive e-mail.

Client-Server Architecture
A network architecture in which each computer or processor on the network is either a **Client** or a **Server** (cf.). Servers are powerful computers or processors dedicated to managing disk drives (file servers), printers (print servers) or network traffic (network servers). Clients are **PCs** or **Workstations** (cf.) on which users run applications. Clients rely on servers for resources such as files, devices and even processing power. Client-server architectures are sometimes called two-tier architectures.

Closure
When a Customer or User is satisfied that an Incident or Problem has been resolved.

Closure Code
The classification of an Incident or Problem after it has been resolved and the true impact, cause or resolution is understood.

Code of Practice
Refers to the BSI publication DISC PD0005 - Code of Practice for IT Service Management.

Cold Stand-by / Start / Site (portable or fixed)
An empty computer room, either in portable accommodation or on a fixed site, with power, environmental control and telecommunications, but no IT equipment or software, for use in an emergency. (cf. *Gradual Recovery*).

Command Bridge
See *Operations Bridge.*

Compliance
See *Auditing for Compliance*.

Component CI
One of the Configuration Items (CIs) forming an *Assembly CI* (cf.).

Component Failure Impact Analysis
A technique developed by IBM which uses a matrix to identify areas of risk in IT service provision by linking the failure of individual Configuration Items (CIs) to their impact on the overall level of service provided.

Computer Telephony Integration
An industry term for the integration of computer systems and telephones. CTI first became available in the 1980s as organisations started using Voicemail, Fax-on-Demand, *Interactive Voice Response* (cf.), *Automatic Call Distribution* (cf.) for inbound calls and Predictive Diallers for outbound telemarketing.

Concurrency
A measure of the number of users engaged in the same operation at the same time - a critical Capacity Planning issue.

Confidentiality
Protection of data from unauthorised access.

Configuration
Any group of Configuration Items (CIs) that need to be controlled in order to deliver IT services.

Configuration and Change Management
An approach that considers integrating Configuration, Change and certain aspects of Release Management into a single function.

Configuration and Change Management Plan
A document describing the combined Configuration and Change Management function, including the organisational roles and responsibilities, the architecture and design of the CMDB, DSL and DHS, and the policies and procedures.

Configuration Audit
A physical check on the infrastructure to determine whether the Configuration Management Database (CMDB) and the physical Configuration Items (CIs) correspond. This could be anything from detecting unauthorised or unlicensed items to checking on the status of an item.

Configuration Baseline
See *Baseline*.

Configuration Control
Activities concerned with ensuring that only authorised and identifiable Configuration Items (CIs) are recorded throughout their life-cycle and that no CI is added, modified, replaced or removed without appropriate controlling documentation, e.g. an approved Request for Change. Configuration Control also includes controlling access to the information held on CIs.

Configuration Identification
The selection, unique identification, description and labelling of assembly and component Configuration Items (CIs), and the relationships between them.

Configuration Item
A Configuration Item (CI) is any component of an IT Infrastructure, including a documentary item such as a Service Level Agreement or a Request For Change, which is (or is to be) under the control of Configuration Management

and therefore subject to formal Change control. The lowest level CI is normally the smallest unit that will be changed independently of other components. CIs may vary widely in complexity, size and type, from an entire service (including all its hardware, software, documentation, etc.) to a single program module or a minor hardware component. All existing or potential service Problems will be capable of being linked to one or more CIs.

Configuration Management

The process of planning for, identifying, controlling and verifying the Configuration Items (CIs) within a service, recording and reporting their status and, in support of Change Management, assessing the potential IT impact of changing those items. (cf. **Configuration Identification, Configuration Control, Configuration Status Accounting, Configuration Verification**).

Configuration Management Database

A database (CMDB) that contains details about the attributes and history of each Configuration Item (CI) and details of the important relationships between CIs. The information held may be in a variety of formats, textual, diagrammatic, photographic, etc.; effectively a data map of the physical reality of IT Infrastructure.

Configuration Management Plan

A document describing the organisation and procedures for the Configuration Management of a specific product, activity or service.

Configuration Management System

A software tool that provides support for Configuration, Change and Release Management.

Configuration Set

A term sometimes used to describe a group of Configuration Items (CIs) that normally belong together. (cf. **Assembly CI, Baseline.**)

Configuration Status Accounting

A task of Configuration Management concerned with recording the state of a Configuration Item (CI) at any point in time, past, present or future.

Configuration Verification

A task of Configuration Management concerned with ensuring that information held on Configuration Items (CIs) in the Configuration Management Database (CMDB) is accurate.

Contingency Plan

See **IT Service Continuity Plan**.

Contingency Planning

See **IT Service Continuity Planning.**

Continuous Availability

A characteristic of an IT service that masks from the users the effects of losses of service, planned or unplanned. (cf. **Continuous Operation**).

Continuous Improvement

A cornerstone of IT Service Management best practice whereby all aspects of service provision are continually challenged to identify potential increases in economy, efficiency or effectiveness.

Continuous Learning, Innovation and Improvement

Organisational performance is maximised when it is based on the management and sharing of knowledge within a culture of continuous learning, innovation and improvement.

Continuous Operation

A characteristic of an IT service that masks from the users the effects of planned downtime. (cf. **Continuous Availability**).

Contract

An understanding, usually in documentary form, between two bodies with separate legal existence, e.g. between an IT services department and an external supplier. Subject to specific legal interpretations. (cf. **Agreement**).

Contract Managers

Responsible for the management of all IT related contracts which are not managed directly by the customer. Their prime responsibility is to ensure that there is coherence between the levels of service offered to customers and those agreed with external suppliers. This includes drafting and reviewing the content of contracts and also regular liaison with suppliers, monitoring the supplier's performance during the contract term.

Control
See *Configuration Control*.

Cost
Amount of expenditure, actual or notional, attributable to a specific activity, service or business unit. When considering pricing, the cost may be the full cost, calculated as a total cost of ownership, including depreciation and planned renewal, or the marginal cost of providing the service now, based upon the investment already made.

Cost Centre
A unit or activity to which costs are allotted. Also, an approach to IT Financial Management where IT is budgeted and there is nominal charging for specific services; it is concerned with both input and output costs.

Cost Effectiveness
See *Effectiveness*.

Cost Element
Within each high level Input Cost Type there will be a number of defined Cost Elements. Typically, People costs will consist of payroll, staff benefits, expenses, overtime, consultancy, etc.

Cost Model
In order to calculate the costs of providing services it is necessary to design and build a framework in which all costs can be recorded and allocated or apportioned to specific Customers or other activities. Such 'Cost Models' can be developed to show, for example, the cost of each service, the cost for each Customer or the cost for each location. The usual start point is to develop a Cost-by-Customer Cost Model.

Cost Plus
A means of pricing, often used when the costs cannot easily be predicted, that adds a percentage to the costs for recovery purposes.

Cost Types (Input)
The categorisation of IT service input costs into types for the purposes of building a Cost Model should aim for simplicity and consistency. Typical Cost Types are hardware, software, people, accommodation, external services and transfer. These are high-level classifications of what money is spent on and each will be sub-divided into a number of Cost Elements.

Cost Unit (Input)
See **Cost Element**.

Cost Unit (Output)
The functional business output cost unit, e.g. invoice, stock picking list, report, for which a charge will be made.

Cost-by-Customer Cost Model
A framework in which costs are identified and allocated or apportioned according to the customers that incur those costs. This model is most commonly used as a basis for charging.

Cost-by-Service Cost Model
A framework in which costs are identified and allocated or apportioned according to the services that are delivered by IT.

Costing
The process of identifying costs and relating them to business units or activities.

Countermeasure
An action taken to reduce risk. It may reduce the 'value' of the asset, the threats facing the asset or the vulnerability of that asset to those threats.

Creativity
The generation of ideas for new or improved working practices, products or services.

Crisis Management
The processes concerned with managing the whole range of impacts following a disaster, including elements such as adverse media coverage and loss of customer confidence.

Critical Success Factors
The certain factors that will be critical to the success of the organisation, in the sense that if the objectives associated with those factors are not achieved, the organisation will fail – perhaps catastrophically so. Identification of CSFs should help determine the strategic objectives of the organisation.

Culture

The total range of behaviours, ethics and values that are transmitted, practised and reinforced by members of the organisation. This might include the way authority is exercised and people are rewarded, the methods of communication used and the degree of formality expected.

Customer

A business manager authorised to negotiate with the IT supplier on behalf of the business. Typically someone who has responsibility for the cost of the service, either directly through charging or indirectly in terms of demonstrable business need. (cf. *Intelligent Customer*). The term must be used carefully because an IT Services organisation's customers will undoubtedly have customers of their own within their Supply Chain.

Customer Focus

Recognising that the customer is the final arbiter of product and service quality and that customer loyalty, retention and market share gain are best optimised through clear focus on the needs of current and potential customers.

Customer Relationship Management

All of the activities necessary to ensure that IT Service Managers have a true understanding of their customers' needs and that the customers also understand their responsibilities. Use of the term in an IT Service Management sense should not be confused with the specific CRM term which generally focused on helping a business 'sell' more to its customers rather than deliver better services.

Database Management System
A management system associated with a structured set of data that allows th
data to be accessed in a variety of ways. In a Relational DBMS, t
relationships between the data elements form keys to reduce the amount
data needing to be held and to improve navigation and access speeds.

Definitive Hardware Store
A location, or a number of locations, set aside for the secure storage
definitive hardware spares maintained at the same level as the equivale
hardware Configuration Items (CIs) in the live environment. Only authorise
hardware should be accepted into the DHS, strictly controlled by Change an
Release Management.

Definitive Software Library
A physical library where all quality-controlled versions of all softwa
Configuration Items (CIs) are held in their definitive form, together with ar
associated CIs such as licence and other documentation. This one logic
storage area may in reality consist of one or more physical software libraries
filestores. They should be separate from development and test filestore area
Only authorised software should be accepted into the DSL, strictly controlle
by Change and Release Management.

Deliverable
An item which must be created as part of a stated requirement. It may be a fin
product or one on which one or more subsequent deliverables are dependent.

Delivering Information Systems to Customers
DISC is the organisation within the British Standards Institution that help
enterprises improve their operational effectiveness by acceleratin
standardisation of information systems and by promoting standards an
making them easier to exploit.

Delta Release
A release that does not replace all component Configuration Items (CIs) with
a release unit, but rather includes only those CIs that have changed since th
last release of the software. Sometimes referred to as a 'partial' release.

Demand Management

Influencing the use of IT capacity, perhaps by incentive or penalty, in circumstances where unmanaged demand is likely to exceed the ability to deliver. Demand Management is achieved by assigning resources according to priorities.

Deming

In his book 'Out of the Crisis', W. Edwards Deming described 14 points that lie at the heart of quality improvement. Since the IT Service Management philosophy is essentially one of continuous improvement, those 14 points apply, and any ITSM initiative that ignores them does so at its peril. They include:

* Constancy of purpose toward improvement of product and service.
* Cease dependence on inspection to achieve quality by building quality into the service.
* Award business on the basis of total cost rather than the 'price tag'.
* Improve constantly and forever the system of production and service, to improve quality and productivity, and thus constantly decrease costs.
* Institute training on the job.
* Institute leadership. The aim of supervision is to help people and machines do a better job.
* Break down barriers between departments. Everyone must work as a team to foresee problems of production and in use that may be encountered with the product or service.
* Institute a vigorous programme of education and self-improvement.
* Put everybody in the organisation to work to accomplish the transformation. The transformation is everybody's job.

Dependency

The direct or indirect reliance of one process or activity upon another.

Depreciation

Depreciation is the measure of the reduction in the useful economic life of a capital item. It will take into account the current value of the asset, the expected remaining length of life and any residual value of the asset at the end of its useful life. Finance departments will give guidance on the method of depreciation to be employed.

Detection

The second stage, after Occurrence, in an Incident life-cycle when the service failure becomes known to the IT service organisation. (cf. *Incident Life-cycle*).

Diagnosis

The third stage, after Detection, in an Incident life-cycle during which the service provider seeks to understand the root cause of the failure. (cf. **Incident Life-cycle**).

Diagnostic Script

A structured set of questions used by Service Desk staff to enable the faster resolution and/or the more accurate assignment of Incidents. Diagnostic scripts will often be provided and maintained by technical staff as one of their Incident Management process responsibilities.

Disaster Recovery

See **IT Service Continuity Management.**

Differential Charging

A charging policy aimed either at dampening demand for a scarce or expensive resource or encouraging the use of spare capacity.

Direct Cost

A cost which can be allocated in full to a product, service, customer, cost centre or business activity. A group of staff dedicated to developing a Customer application is an example.

Disaster Recovery Planning

The processes within Business Continuity Management that focus upon recovery from, principally, physical disasters.

Discounted Cash Flow

A means of evaluating the future net cash flows generated by a capital project by discounting them to their present-day value. Two methods commonly employed are the 'yield method', where the calculation determines a percentage Internal Rate of Return (IRR) and the 'Net Present Value (NPV) method', where a given discount rate will generate sums of money for comparison.

Do Nothing

An IT Service Continuity Planning option that, positively, decides to take no additional technical or managerial action to reduce the impact of a disastrous loss of service, other, perhaps, than to take out an insurance policy. Because of the importance of most IT services this is rarely an option exercised (except by default!).

Document

Information in readable form, including computer data, which is created or received and maintained as evidence of the service provider's intentions. Records are distinguished from documents by the fact that they function as evidence of activities, rather that evidence of intentions. Examples include policy statements, plans, procedures, Service Level Agreements and contracts. (cf. *Record*).

Domain

See *IT Infrastructure.*

Dormant Contract

A contract in which a supplier agrees, perhaps for a premium, to supply a product or service on demand, usually in response to an unplanned event.

Downtime

The total period that a service or component is not operational within an agreed service time. Measured from when a service or component fails to when normal operations recommence.

Duplex

Duplex equipment provides two, usually identical, IT components each of which is capable of performing the full task if the other fails.

Economy

Economy is one of the measures needed to determine value for money. It concerns the cost of the inputs to an activity; the resources needed to deliver a service. Typical measures will include money, time, people and quality. (cf. *Effectiveness, Efficiency, Value for Money*).

Effectiveness

Effectiveness, or Cost Effectiveness, is one of the measures needed to determine value for money. It concerns the cost of the outputs from an activity and the conformance of those outputs to a specification or need. Typical measures will include money, time, people and quality. Any investment that increases the cost of providing IT services should result in an enhancement to service quality or quantity. If this is not so, then the business case must be quite clear about why the Change is necessary. (cf. *Economy, Efficiency, Value for Money*).

Efficiency

Efficiency is one of the measures needed to determine value for money. It concerns the ratio of inputs (economy) to outputs (effectiveness) and is sometimes referred to as 'bangs per buck'. Typical measures will include money, time, people and quality. (cf. *Economy, Effectiveness, Value for Money*).

Electronic Data Interchange

Direct computer-to-computer transfer of business information, which aims to reduce paper consumption, eliminate data entry errors, speed up transfer of business information and facilitate 'Just in Time' processes.

Emergency Change

A Change planned, scheduled and implemented at very short notice in order to protect a service from an unacceptable risk of failure or degradation, lack or loss of functionality.

End-User / User

One whose business responsibilities are aided or supported by the use of an IT service.

Environment

An assembly of computers, communication facilities, procedures, etc. that work together to provide a discrete type of service. There may be one or more environments on a physical platform, e.g. test and production. An environment has unique features and characteristics that dictate how it may be administered in a similar, yet diverse, manner. The term is also used to describe physical environments in terms of their accommodation, air conditioning, etc.

Equity

Sometimes referred to as the fourth 'E' alongside Economy, Effectiveness and Efficiency, Equity is concerned with ensuring that the extent and costs of services are fairly divided among the recipients.

Error

See *Known Error.*

Error Control

One of the tasks of Problem Management, Error Control encompasses identifying, recording, classifying and progressing Known Errors. Error Control extends to the promotion of Changes and the completion of the resolution phase i.e. the confirmed successful implementation of an amended or replacement Configuration Item (CI) that leads to closure of the linked Problem and Known Error records.

Escalation

Passing information and/or requesting action on an Incident, Problem or Change to more senior staff (hierarchical escalation) or other specialists (functional escalation). The circumstances in which either vertical escalation or information/authority to apply further resources or horizontal escalation or greater functional involvement need to be precisely described, so that the purpose of the escalation and the nature of the required response is absolutely clear to all parties as the escalation occurs. Escalation rules will be geared to priority targets. Functional escalation is sometimes called referral.

Estimation

Estimation is the cheapest and least accurate form of modelling. This is where an educated guess is taken as to the performance of a specific scenario.

Ethics

The universal morals that an organisation adopts and abides by.

European Foundation for Quality Management
See *British Quality Foundation.*

Examen Instituut
EXIN is the Dutch examination board for informatics. (cf. *Informatio Systems Examination Board*).

Excellence
Outstanding practice in managing the organisation and achieving result based on fundamental concepts which will include: results orientatio customer focus; leadership and constancy of purpose; processes and fact involvement of people; continuous improvement and innovation; mutuall beneficial partnership; public responsibility. Excellence can only be measure effectively by objective comparison with external best practice.

Exception Reporting
Reducing the Management Information produced to that which most demand or deserves attention. The 'Top Ten' style of list is an example.

Expert User
See *Super User.*

External Customers
The customers outside of the organisation. These may also include othe customers in the chain of distribution. In an outsourced situation, externa customers often refers to those outside the scope of the contract but still withi the organisation.

External Measure
See *External Target.*

External Service Costs
An input Cost Type that represents complex mixtures of services bought i from third parties.

External Specsheet
A working document that enables the Service Level Management (SLM function to detail exactly what service must be delivered to the Customer.

External Target
A measure of a delivered service, expressed in terms that reflect the benefi delivered to the Customer's business.

Failure

A Failure occurs when a functional unit is no longer fit for purpose.

Fault

A condition that causes a functional unit to fail to perform the required function.

Fault Tolerance

The ability of a service to continue when a failure occurs. (cf. *Resilience*).

Fault Tree Analysis

A technique, using Boolean notation, of identifying the chain of events leading to an adverse impact on services.

Financial Management for IT Services

The Service Management process of budgeting, accounting and charging for IT services.

First Level Support

The technical and managerial resources within the Service Desk available at the initial point of contact with the Customer/User.

First Time Fix Rate

A commonly used metric that measures the proportion of Incidents resolved at the first point of contact between a User and a Service Desk, without delay or referral.

Fishbone Diagram

See *Cause/Effect Diagram.*

Fixed Cost

A cost that does not vary with usage or throughput of work. Examples are a standard term maintenance contract for a server or a corporate software licence (within agreed User limits).

Fixed Price

A price agreed with a Customer for a given period and based upon a predicted consumption.

Follow the Sun Support
A Service Desk organisation that provides 24-hour support using Service Desks located in various countries. Calls are logged in one location and then passed to, or picked up by, the next location when the originating office closes.

Fortress Approach
An approach to IT Service Continuity where the entire IT site is made as disaster-proof as possible.

Forward Schedule of Change
A schedule that contains details of all the Changes approved for implementation and their proposed implementation dates. It should be agreed with Customers, Service Level Management, the Service Desk and Availability Management. Once agreed, the Service Desk would communicate to the Users any planned or additional downtime arising from implementing the Changes (cf. *Projected Service Availability*).

Front-office / Front-end
The business processes relating to Customer interaction, often including marketing, pricing and sales related functions.

Full Absorption Costing
A principle where all direct costs are allocated to cost units and overhead costs are apportioned according to a meaningful algorithm that attempts to reflect probable resource usage.

Full Cost
The total cost of all the resources used in supplying a service, including the direct costs, a share of indirect costs and any marketing, selling and distribution, etc. costs. All cash and non-cash costs, for example the cost of capital and, where appropriate, planned renewal costs, are included. Full costs are required to calculate the Total Cost of Ownership (cf. *Cost, Total Cost of Ownership*).

Full Release
A release that tests, distributes and implements all components of a release unit, regardless of whether or not they have changed since the last release of the software.

Function

The actions or intended purpose of a person, team or thing in a specific role. Service Management functions may be considered as high-level business activities, often with a broad scope and associated with a particular job, consisting of a collection of lower level activities. The characteristics of a function are that it is continuous and represents a defining aspect of the business enterprise. It is usually associated with more than one process and contributes to the execution of those processes. Rarely do (or should) functions mirror the organisational structure.

Functional Escalation

See *Escalation*.

Going Rate
A means of pricing where the price is comparable with that charged by othe internal departments or similar organisations.

Gradual Recovery
This IT Service Continuity option provides for the recovery of IT services i support of business processes that can function without their full IT support f 72 hours or more. Sometimes known as 'Cold Stand-by/Start', this option wi typically make provision for empty accommodation (portable or static) full equipped with power, environmental controls, a local network cablin infrastructure and telecommunications connections. The necessary hardware ar software will need to be installed. (cf. *Immediate Recovery, Intermediat Recovery*).

Graphical User Interface
Designed to make programs easier to use, GUIs can free the User fro learning complex command languages. GUIs such as those used by Window and Apple Macintosh typically feature a pointer, a pointing device, icons, desktop, windows and menus.

H

Hard Charging
The situation within an enterprise whereby funds are transferred from the Customers to the service provider in payment for the delivery of services.

Help Desk
An interface, often referred to as a 'Single Point of Contact', between IT and its Users. Its core processes are Incident Management and the management of User requests, ensuring that no call or Incident is lost, forgotten or ignored and that service is returned as quickly as possible. (cf. **Service Desk**).

Hierarchical Escalation
See **Escalation**.

Hot Stand-by / Start / Site (internal, external or mobile)
An IT Service Continuity option - either provided from within the organisation or by a 3rd party, possibly in a fixed place or mobile, consisting of a computer room with full environmental and telecommunications facilities plus the necessary hardware and software to enable the site to take over processing from the normal infrastructure with minimal disruption to services. (cf. **Immediate Recovery, Intermediate Recovery**).

Identification
See **Configuration Identification**

Immediate Recovery
In literal terms, this IT Service Continuity option provides for the immediate recovery of services in a contingency situation. The instant availability of services distinguishes this option from what may be referred to as 'Hot Stand-by/Start', which typically will permit services to be recovered within 2 to 24 hours depending on the criticality of the business process they support. Depending on that business criticality, 'immediate' recovery may therefore vary from zero to 24 hours. (cf. **Gradual Recovery, Intermediate Recovery**).

Impact
A measure of the effect that an Incident, Problem or Change is having or might have on the business being provided with IT services. Often equal to the extent to which agreed or expected levels of service may be distorted. Together with urgency, and perhaps technical severity, it is the major means of assigning priority for dealing with Incidents, Problems or Changes.

Impact Analysis
The identification of critical business processes and the potential damage or loss that may be caused to the organisation resulting from a disruption to those processes, or perhaps from a proposed change. Business impact analysis identifies the form the loss or damage will take; how that degree of damage or loss is likely to escalate with time following an Incident; the minimum staffing, facilities and services needed to enable business processes to continue to operate at a minimum acceptable level; and the time within which they should be recovered. The time within which full recovery of the business processes is to be achieved is also identified.

Impact Code
A simple code assigned to Incidents, Problems and Changes reflecting the degree of actual or potential impact on Customers' business activities. Also the extent of deterioration in normal User service levels. An impact code is not necessarily fixed and may change to reflect changing circumstances.

Impact Scenario

An IT Service Continuity Management term describing the type of impact on the business that could follow a business disruption. It will usually be related to a business process and will always refer to a period of time, e.g. Customer services will be unable to operate for two days.

Incident

An event which is not part of the standard operation of a service and which causes or may cause disruption to or a reduction in the quality of services and Customer productivity.

An Incident might give rise to the identification and investigation of a Problem, but never becomes a Problem. Even if handed over to the Problem Management process for 2nd Line Incident Control it remains an Incident. Problem Management might, however, manage the resolution of the Incident and Problem in tandem, for instance if the Incident can only be closed by resolution of the Problem.

Incident Categorisation

A sub-division of Classification, which provides a means of identifying, using a series of structured codes, firstly, what appears to have gone wrong with the IT Service (the symptoms), secondly why (the cause of that failure) and thirdly identification of the component likely to be at fault. The category codes are elements within the classification data string (see **Classification**) and are essential for fault analysis purposes.

Incident Classification

See **Classification**.

Incident Control

The process of identifying, recording, classifying and progressing Incidents until the affected service is restored. The collection of data to identify causes of Incidents is a secondary objective of Incident Control, though this may sometimes be necessary to effect Incident resolution. Incident Control is essentially a task of Incident Management, and therefore of the Service Desk, but it may occasionally extend beyond the defined role or authority of that group and require the 2nd Line support of other staff, possibly Problem Management. The exact circumstance under which this happens would be described in an Incident Management procedure.

Incident Control Support

This is an occasional task, perhaps undertaken by the Problem Management team. There are instances when an Incident has occurred and it becomes apparent that further time and resource investment by Service Desk staff (both 1st and 2nd Level) is likely to impact upon their prime responsibility of responding to Customers and returning services as quickly as possible. These are situations that call for detailed investigation and diagnosis, that require the co-ordination of technical support team(s), or that cater for the re-direction of Service Desk resources elsewhere (e.g. to other Incidents). Another group, such as Problem Management, may in these circumstances be asked to manage the operational progress of the Incident. However, the Service Desk retain their overall responsibility for the Incident's life-cycle management. Such an Incident would be referred to the Incident Control Support group by Incident Management in accordance with Incident Management procedures.

Incident Life-cycle

The progression of an incident through Occurrence of the Incident, Detection of the Incident, Diagnosis of the cause of failure, Repair of the CI, Recovery of the CI back into the live infrastructure and Restoration of service.

Incident Management

The Service Management process of managing unexpected operational events with the primary objective of returning service to Customers as quickly as possible.

Incident Record

A record containing the details and history of an Incident.

Incident Report

A form, or screen, containing details of Incidents involving any component of an IT Infrastructure or any aspect of the IT service. Incident reports may come from a variety of sources and will usually result in the creation of an Incident record.

Indirect Cost

A cost incurred which cannot be directly allocated in full to a single product, service, Customer, cost centre or business activity; incurred on behalf of a number of cost units or centres to which the cost may be apportioned. An example would be the costs of a server used to support three separate services.

Information and Communications Technology

Information Technology, with the role of telecommunications technology emphasised. (cf. *Information Technology*).

Information Service

All of the components that form an IT service supporting a Customer's business process, including not only the computing and telecommunications hardware and software but the people, processes and supporting documentation, training, etc. (cf. *Information Technology Service*).

Information System

The hardware and software (mainly) that lies at the heart of an IT Service supporting a Customer's business process.

Information Systems Examination Board

The UK ISEB, part of the British Computer Society, administers and awards IT qualifications, including the Foundation, Practitioner's and Manager's Certificates in IT Service Management. It is one of a number of bodies worldwide that offer equivalent examinations in IT Service Management.

Information Technology

The application of science to the processing of data according to programmed instructions in order to derive results. In the widest sense, IT includes all information and all technology; in a much narrower sense, telecommunications technology is excluded – or for some particular reason needs to be emphasised. cf. *Information and Communications Technology*).

Information Technology Service

A set of related functions provided by IT systems in support of one or more business areas, which in turn may be made up of software, hardware and communications facilities, perceived by the Customer as a coherent and self-contained entity. An IT service may range from access to a single application, such as a general ledger system, to a complex set of facilities including many applications, as well as office automation, that might be spread across a number of hardware and software platforms. (cf. *Information Service*).

Informed Customer

See *Intelligent Customer.*

Infrastructure

From an IT Service Management perspective, the term is used to describe all of the components (Configuration Items) employed in the delivery of IT services to users, including the computing and telecommunications hardware, software, accommodation, people, documentation and meta-data. From a business perspective, the infrastructure is a shared resource, the state of which bounds the adaptability and change capacity of the enterprise.

Infrastructure Service

A service provided by IT to enable the delivery of business services, but not themselves directly adding value to business processes. Normally treated as an overhead cost, although the overhead might be absorbed by specific business services. The provision of corporate-wide desktop facilities is a typical example of an infrastructure service, the provision of general strategic technological advice another.

Innovation

The practical translation of ideas into new or improved products, services, processes, systems or social interactions.

Input Cost Types

See **Cost Types (Input)**.

Integration Testing

Putting together all of the components, including the hardware and software involved in a Change, as they will exist in the live infrastructure, to ensure that they work together.

Integrity

Completeness and soundness. Maintaining these will require the protection of data from unauthorised Change. Also the consistency of data and linkage between data in a database (referential integrity).

Intelligent Customer

A term used to describe the situation where a Customer of IT services has all of the abilities to enable the successful planning, specification, acquisition, implementation and use of IS/IT to achieve business objectives at best value for money. Also referred to an 'Informed Customer'.

Interactive Processing

Processing that involves accepting input from a human. Interactive computer systems are programs that allow Users to enter data or commands. Most popular programs, such as word processors or spreadsheet applications are interactive. Non-interactive processing, such as **Batch Processing** (cf.) requires no further end-user contact once started.

Interactive Voice Response

A form of Automatic Call Distribution that uses computing and telecommunications technology to provide callers, in the better applications, with choice and control over the routing of their call. Although disliked by some, particularly the poorly designed systems, a growing proportion of callers now expect to be able to transact business through an IVR system when they choose to do so. Although some calls are undoubtedly more suited to 'live' interaction, at other times IVR may be more appropriate because it allows Customers to complete transactions faster, at any time of the day or night, without having to wait in a queue.

Interface

Physical or functional interaction at the boundary between Configuration Items (CIs).

Intermediate Recovery

Alternatively known as 'Warm Stand-by/Start', this IT Service Continuity option typically provides for the recovery of services in a contingency situation within 24 to 72 hours. It is used by organisations that need to recover IT facilities within a predetermined time in order to prevent business processes being severely impacted by the failure. (cf. **Gradual Recovery, Immediate Recovery**).

Internal Measure

See **Internal Target.**

Internal Specsheet

A working document that enables the Service Level Management (SLM) function to detail exactly what the IT department and its suppliers must do to deliver a service to a Customer.

Internal Target
One of the measures against which supporting processes for the IT service are compared. Usually expressed in technical terms relating directly to the underpinning service being measured.

Internet Protocol
Originally specified in 1981 for the Defense Advanced Research Projects Agency (DARPA), the Internet Protocol (IP) is designed for use in interconnected systems of packet-switched computer communication networks. The IP provides for transmitting blocks of data called datagrams from sources to destinations, where sources and destinations are hosts identified by fixed length addresses. The IP also provides for fragmentation and reassembly of long datagrams, if necessary, for transmission through 'small packet' networks.

Inventory Management
A subset of Configuration Management that focuses on the management (control and financial accounting) of the most expensive or attractive Configuration Items in the IT infrastructure. (cf. *Asset Management, Configuration Management*).

Investment Appraisal
The process of determining what financial benefits might arise from investing in changes to IT service quality or quantity. (cf. *Capital Investment Appraisal*).

Invocation
In IT Service Continuity Management terms, the initiation of the disaster recovery process.

Invocation and Recovery Phase
The second phase of a business recovery plan.

Invocation of Business Recovery Plans
Putting business recovery plans into operation after a business disruption.

Invocation of Stand-by Arrangements
Putting stand-by arrangements into operation as part of business recovery activities.

Invoicing
see *Billing*.

Ishikawa Diagram
see *Cause / Effect Diagram.*

ISO 9000
Guidelines and assurance of process and procedure standards for quality assurance systems. The current version of ISO 9000 is ISO 9000:2000.

IT Accounting
The set of processes that enable the IT organisation to fully account for the way its money is spent.

IT Accounting System
A set of interrelated activities, policies and tools, which is used to budget, track and charge for IT services.

IT Availability Metrics Model
A framework used to measure the availability, reliability, maintainability and response time of a service for several categories of infrastructure, application and Customer.

IT Infrastructure
All of the components (Configuration Items) that are needed to deliver IT services to customers. The IT Infrastructure consists of more than just hardware and software.

IT Infrastructure Library
The collection of volumes produced by the UK Office of Government Commerce (previously CCTA) that describe IT Service Management best practice. The library is intended to assist organisations to provide quality IT service in the face of budgetary constraints, skill shortages, system complexity, rapid change, current and future User requirements and growing User expectations.

Originally produced in the late 80s – early 90s as a set of more than forty volumes, at the heart of the latest issue of the library is a set of six books: **Service Support** and **Service Delivery** provide advice on how to manage the core processes of IT Service Management; **Planning to Implement Service Management** explains the steps necessary to identify how an

organisation might expect to benefit from ITIL, and how to set about reapir
those benefits; **ICT Infrastructure Management** covers Network Servic
Management, Operations Management, Management of Local Processor
Computer Installation and Acceptance, and for the first time, System
Management; and **Applications Management** embraces the Softwa
Development Lifecycle, expanding the issues touched on in Software Lifecyc
Support and Testing of IT Services. **Applications Management** al
provides more detail on Business Change with emphasis being placed on cle
requirement definition and implementation of solutions. Finally, **Th
Business Perspective** volume deals with fully understanding the nature
IT service provision and covers Business Continuity Managemen
Partnerships and Outsourcing, Surviving Change and Transformation
Business Practices through Radical Change. (cf. *Service Suppor
Service Delivery*).

IT Service
A set of related components provided in support of one or more busine
processes. The service will comprise a range of Configuration Item (CI) Typ
but will be perceived by Customers and Users as a self-contained, sing
coherent entity.

IT Service Continuity Management
The process of assessing and managing risks to IT services by examinin
Configuration Item (CI) values, threats and vulnerabilities, developin
appropriate countermeasures, creating an IT Service Continuity plan, a
managing any disaster situations that occur. (cf. *Business Continuit
Management*).

IT Service Continuity Plan
A plan detailing actions and procedures to be followed by IT in the event o
disaster (cf. *Business Continuity Planning*).

IT Service Continuity Planning
The process of developing, testing and maintaining a plan for use in the eve
of a disaster - a subset of IT Service Continuity Management (cf. *Busine
Continuity Planning*).

IT Service Management
The principles and practices of designing, delivering and maintaining
services, to an agreed level of quality, in support of a Customer activity.

IT Service Management Forum

Founded in the UK in 1991, the itSMF is the only internationally recognised and independent body dedicated to professional IT Service Management. It is a not-for-profit organisation, wholly owned and principally operated by its membership. Originally formed as the IT Infrastructure Management Forum (ITIMF), the name was changed in 1997 in order to reflect more accurately the organisation's focus. There are active national 'chapters' of itSMF throughout the world.

The itSMF is a major influence on and contributor to Industry Best Practices and Standards worldwide, working in partnership with such organisations as OGC (the UK Government advisory body), the British Standards Institution (BSi) and a number of national and international Examination Boards.

Iterative Activities

This term refers to the activities of Monitoring, Analysing, Tuning and Implementing that form the day-to-day management of performance within Capacity Management.

Job Description

Agreed written statement of the tasks to be undertaken for a given post, often including, responsibilities, knowledge/skill requirements and measures of success.

Kepner-Tregoe Analysis

A problem analysis technique that identifies five stages; defining, describing, establishing possible causes, testing the most probable cause and verifying the true cause.

Key Performance Indicator

A measure (quantitative or qualitative) that enables the overall delivery of a service to be assessed by both business and IT representatives. KPIs should be few in number and focus on the service's potential contribution to business success. To be effective in improving business performance, they must be linked to a strategic plan which details how the business intends to accomplish its vision and mission. The metrics selected must address all aspects of performance results, describe the targeted performance in measurable terms and be deployed to the organisational level that has the authority, resources and knowledge to take the necessary action.

Key Success Factors

See *Critical Success Factors.*

Knowledge

Knowledge is part of the hierarchy made up of data, information and knowledge. Data are raw facts. Information is data with context and perspective. Knowledge is information with guidance for action based upon insight and experience.

Knowledge Base

Data repository holding information on Incidents, Problems and Known Errors, enabling an organisation to match new Incidents against previous ones and thus to reuse established solutions and approaches.

Known Error

A fault in a Configuration Item (CI) identified by the successful diagnosis of a Problem and for which a temporary work-around or a permanent solution has been identified.

The link between the Known Error and the CI may arise from local diagnos
of a Problem but may equally be derived from an external source of Know
Errors. It is important that all relevant Known Errors are recorded in t
Configuration Management Database (CMDB) although, clearly, the CMD
will not be the only source of Known Error data. Since many Problems w
have multiple causes, the links between individual Problems and individu
Known Errors might be complex.

Known Error Classification
See *Classification.*

Known Error Database
The database containing the recorded solutions of all internal and possib
some external Known Errors; sometimes called a Known Error Log or KEL.

Known Error Record
A record containing the details and history of a Known Error.

Known Error Report
A form or screen which formally records a deviation from specification, as
consequence of identifying a Known Error, e.g. during Incident or Proble
Management.

Leaders
The people who co-ordinate and balance the interests of all those with a stake in the organisation, including the executive team, all other managers and those in team leadership positions or with a subject leadership role.

Leadership and Constancy of Purpose
The behaviour of an organisation's leaders creates a clarity and unity of purpose within the organisation and an environment in which the organisation and its people can excel.

Learning
The acquiring and understanding of information, which may lead to improvement or change. Examples of organisational learning activities include benchmarking, internally and externally led assessments and/or audits, and best practice studies. Examples of individual learning include training and professional qualifications.

Licence Management
Controlling and auditing the use of licensed software within an organisation. Configuration or Asset Management allows the tracking of software usage from ordering through to disposal.

Life-cycle
Analogising a product or process to something alive - treating the stages as elements of its life. By defining identifiable, discrete stages, moving through that life-cycle can be done in a controlled manner.

Live Build Environment
An IT system or discrete part of an IT system (made up of hardware and system software) which is used to build software releases for live use.

Live Environment
An IT system or discrete part of an IT system (made up of hardware and system software) which is used to run software that is in live use, and sometimes to build software releases for live use. Also commonly referred to as a Production Environment. Access to the Live Environment should be restricted to authorised staff.

Local Area Network

A computer network that spans a relatively small area. Most LANs are confined to a single building or group of buildings but may be connected together through a **Wide Area Network** (cf.). LANs allow many Users to share the more expensive devices, such as colour laser printers, as well as data. Users can also use the LAN to communicate with each other, by, for example, sending e-mail.

Mainframe Computer

A very large and expensive computer capable of supporting hundreds, or even thousands, of users simultaneously. The distinction between the smaller types of mainframes and Minicomputers (cf.) is difficult to define. It really depends on how the manufacturer chooses to market its machines.

Maintainability

The ability of a component or an IT service, under stated conditions of use, to be retained in, or restored to, a state in which it can perform its required functions. Maintainability also describes maintenance being performed under stated conditions and using prescribed procedures and resources.

Major Incident

An Incident where the impact on the business is extreme.

Management by Process and Facts

Organisations perform more effectively when all inter-related activities are understood and systematically managed and decisions concerning current operations and planned improvements are made using reliable information that includes stakeholder perceptions.

Management Information

Simplistically, exactly what it says. However, true MI is used, indeed needed, to make informed decisions and much of what is produced and referred to as MI is useless for that purpose. The repetitive production of data that appears to meet no specific management need should therefore always be vigorously questioned.

Management System

The framework of processes and procedures used to ensure that the organisation can fulfil all tasks required to achieve its objectives.

Manual Back-up

See *Clerical Back-up.*

Manual Workaround

A temporary, non-IT based, resolution to an Incident or Problem.

Marginal Cost
The cost of producing one more unit of output after the production system has been established. For example, the cost of generating one printed sheet, i.e. paper and toner, after a laser printer has been purchased and commissioned. (cf. **Cost**).

Market Price
The price is the same as that which would normally be charged by an (another) external supplier.

Maturity Level
An identifiable stage, defined in terms of process features, towards achieving a mature process.

Mean Time Between Failures
MTBF is the mean elapsed time from the time an IT service or component is fully restored until the next occurrence of a failure in the same service or component.

Mean Time Between System / Service Incidents
MTBSI is the mean elapsed time between the occurrence of one system or service failure and the next.

Mean Time To Fix
A term occasionally used to denote the average elapsed time from the occurrence of an incident to the repair of the failed component (the service will probably still not be available to Users).

Mean Time To Repair
MTTR is the mean elapsed time from the occurrence of an Incident to the restoration of service.

Method
A way of doing things in a regular, systematic and orderly fashion.

Metric
Measurable element of a service, process or function. The real value of metrics is seen in their change over time. Reliance on a single metric is not advised, especially if it has the potential to affect User behaviour in an undesirable way.

Minicomputer

A mid-sized computer, perhaps capable of supporting from 4 to about 200 simultaneous Users. In terms of size and power, minicomputers lie between *Workstations* (cf.) and *Mainframes* (cf.).

Mission

A statement that explains the 'raison d'être' of an organisation. It describes why the business or function exists. It is quite distinct from the organisation's objectives, which will indicate how the mission is to be achieved and that achievement measured.

Modelling

A set of tools and techniques used to predict the performance of a specified system under a given volume and variety of work. Modelling is used to predict the availability and performance of services. (cf. *Analytical Modelling, Simulation Modelling*).

Multivoting

A Problem Management technique used to help reduce a large number of items (e.g. a list of themes or the results of Brainstorming) to a manageable few (usually three to five). The technique allows the 'list reduction' to be accomplished quickly and with a high degree of group agreement and eliminates individuals' close identification with particular items.

nth-line Support

A group who are performing a higher level of support call in another group to assist them.

Notional Charging

A technique whereby a Customer is informed of what the charge would be for the service used, although no actual funds change hands; often used as a stage in the introduction of full charging to an organisation.

Objective

A future measurable achievement, usually in support of a more general aim or goal.

Occurrence

The first stage in an Incident life-cycle when the loss of service or loss of service quality occurs. Occurrence precedes Detection.

Office of Government Commerce

The UK Government Department that incorporates the organisation previously known as CCTA. OGC owns the copyright to the IT Infrastructure Library (ITIL) on behalf of the Crown.

Operational

The lowest of the three levels of planning and delivery (Strategic, Tactical, Operational). Involved with actual delivery and execution of the processes and procedures.

Operational / Production Acceptance

The process of ensuring the readiness of operational support capabilities during the transition of a Change from the development to the live environment. This may include ensuring that documentation and procedures are in place and that all Service Management elements such as capacity, service level and disaster recovery needs have been considered.

Operational Costs

Sometimes referred to as Revenue or Running Costs, these are the costs resulting from the day-to-day running of an organisation, e.g. staff costs, hardware maintenance and electricity. The value of the item purchased will diminish as it is used up, e.g. consultancy. Sometimes operational costs are a variable cost (paper, consultancy assistance) and sometimes fixed (salaries). For practical purposes in IT Accounting, operational costs can be considered as those charged to a single financial year, with no depreciation element.

Operational Level Agreement

An internal document, owned by the Service Management Team, that defines the working relationship between different functional areas within an organisation. The OLA sets out the responsibilities for the support and delivery of IT services to Customers. Between a Service Desk and 2nd level support/software maintenance/network management it may be mainly concerned with the activities that must take place should a service fail. In other circumstances, for example in support of Change Management, it is likely to describe the various executive responsibilities and activities of the parties involved. The terms of any OLA must support the qualitative and quantitative statements contained in the Service Charter, Service Level Objectives (SLOs) and Service Level Agreements (SLAs). There is a strong relationship between OLAs and procedures.

Operations Bridge
The combination in one physical location of computer operations, network control (and sometimes the Help Desk or Service Desk).

Opportunity Cost
The value of a benefit sacrificed in favour of an alternative course of action, i.e. the net revenue between that actually obtained and the maximum achievable from any of the possible uses of the relevant resources. For example, there is an opportunity cost associated with using re-cycled paper.

Outsourcing
Where functions previously performed by an organisation are supplied under contract from a third party.

Overheads
The total of indirect materials, wages and expenses.

Ownership
A general term, signifying principal responsibility, which can apply to any activity or event. Incident Management will be 'owned' by the Process Owner (cf.), the Incident itself will be 'owned' by the Service Desk and the failed Configuration Item may be 'owned' by the Customer.

Package Release

A set of software and/or hardware release units that are tested and introduced into the live environment together.

Pain Factor

Sometimes referred to as 'Pain Value', the impact of a particular type of incident or Problem (usually recurring) together with how frequently it occurs and what it would cost to fix it as opposed to living with it.

Pareto Principle / Analysis

The concept that, in many situations, some 80% of the outputs will be generated by only 20% of the inputs. For example, 20% of users will make 80% of the calls to a Service Desk. This principle can be applied in many situations, Problem Management for example, to identify the areas of an organisation or process that will deliver the maximum benefit when improved or when faults or weaknesses are addressed.

Partnership

A working relationship between two or more parties creating added value for the Customer and, often, sharing risks and profits. Partners can include suppliers, distributors, joint ventures, and alliances. However, external suppliers may not always be recognised as formal partners.

Partnership Development

An organisation works more effectively when it has mutually beneficial relationships, built on trust, sharing of knowledge and integration, with its partners.

PD0005

The formal reference number of the BSI publication *A Code of Practice for IT Service Management*.

PD0015

The formal reference number of the BSI publication *A Self-Assessment Workbook for IT Service Management*.

People
All of the individuals employed by the organisation including full time, part time, temporary and contract employees. The term may also include Customers, Users and contractors.

People Development and Involvement
The full potential of an organisation's people is best released through shared values and a culture of trust and empowerment, which encourages the involvement of everyone.

Perception
The opinion of an individual or group of people.

Performance
A measure of attainment achieved by an individual, team, organisation or process.

Performance Management
The task of ensuring that technical resources in the infrastructure provide the best possible value for money and that they are behaving in the manner assumed or described in technical documentation.

Personal Computer
A small, relatively inexpensive computer designed for an individual User although PCs are commonly linked together to form a network. In terms of power, there is great variety. At the high end, there is little distinction between PCs and *Workstations* (cf.).

Post Implementation Review
One or more reviews held after the implementation of a Change to determine, initially, if the Change has been implemented successfully and, subsequently, if the expected benefits have been obtained.

Pricing
Establishing the policy and setting agreed rates for charging customers.

Priority

The value given to an Incident, Problem or Change to indicate its relative importance in order to ensure the appropriate allocation of resources and to determine the timeframe within which action is required. Priority is based upon a coherent and up-to-date understanding of business impact and urgency and, sometimes, technical severity.

Proactive Problem Management

The task of identifying and resolving Problems and Known Errors before Incidents occur.

Problem

The unknown root cause of one or more existing or potential Incidents. Problems may sometimes be identified because of multiple Incidents that exhibit common symptoms. Problems can also be identified from a single significant Incident, indicative of a single error, for which the cause is unknown. Occasionally Problems will be identified well before any related Incidents occur.

Problem Classification

See *Classification.*

Problem Control

The process of identifying, recording, classifying and progressing Problems through investigation and diagnosis until either 'Known Error' status is achieved or an alternative procedural reason for the Problem is revealed.

Problem Management

The Service Management process that encompasses Problem Control, Error Control and the production of Management Information. Problem Management is a process that identifies the root cause of defects, actual and potential. The primary objective is to make sure services are stable, timely and accurate and that Problems neither occur nor recur. Process maturity is denoted by its ability to focus on problem prevention.

Problem Record

A record of the details and history of a Problem.

Problem Report

A form, or screen, containing details of Problems with any component of an IT Infrastructure or any aspect of the IT service.

Procedure

A set of specific steps that describe how an activity should be carried out, and by whom. For example, the procedure dealing with carrying out a post-implementation review of a Change would be likely to describe the scope of the procedure (to what Changes does this procedure apply), its purpose and how the success of the Change will be measured, the individual procedural steps and the responsibilities for carrying out or being involved in each of those steps. Procedures may be supported by more detailed **Work Instructions.**

Process

A process is a series of related activities aimed at achieving a set of objectives in a measurable, usually repeatable, manner. It will have defined information inputs and outputs, will consume resources and will be subject to management controls over time, cost and quality. It will also need to balance benefits against risks. A process defines what is to be achieved; procedures define how the objectives are to be achieved.

Process Control

The task of planning and regulating a process, with the objective of performing it in an efficient, effective and consistent manner.

Process Manager

The Process Manager is responsible for the execution of a process. This role includes operating the defined and agreed process, ensuring it interfaces with all other relevant process, target setting, process audits, effectiveness and efficiency reviews and managing the process improvement cycle. Management of a process is separate from the execution of that process.

Process Maturity

An indication of how close a process is to being developed and complete, and capable of continuous improvement through quantitative measure and feedback.

Process Owner

A Process Owner is a senior manager with overall responsibility for ensuring the suitability of a process. The Process Owner's responsibilities include those of sponsorship, design (including relevant metrics for the process) and operation, mainly quality assurance of continuing process suitability.

Production Environment

See **Live Environment.**

Profit Centre

IT is run as a business with profit objectives. Typically, a type of IT organisation that acts as a business in its own right, although its objectives are set by the organisation as a whole.

Program

An organised list of instructions that, when executed, causes a computer to behave in a predetermined manner. Programs contain variables representing numeric data, text or graphical images and statements that instruct the computer what to do with the variables.

Programme

A portfolio of projects and other activities that are planned, initiated and managed in a co-ordinated way in order to achieve a set of defined business objectives.

Project

A temporary organisation created for the purpose of delivering one or more business products according to a specified business case.

Project Evaluation Review

A review carried out, normally at the end of a project, to confirm whether or not, and if not in what respect, a project attained its specified objectives.

Projected Service Availability

A document used in Change Management to outline the effect of Changes on the levels of availability defined in the Service Level Agreements (SLAs). This document is linked to the Forward Schedule of Change (FSC).

Projects IN Controlled Environments

PRINCE® is an easily tailored and scaleable process-based project management method covering the organisation, management and control of projects. Each process is defined with its key inputs and outputs together with the specific objectives to be achieved and activities to be carried out.

Although PRINCE was originally developed for the needs of UK Government IT projects, the method has since become widely used on both IT and non-IT projects throughout the world. The latest version of the method, PRINCE2, provides a common language for all the parties involved in a project. The method demands a business case that describes the organisation's justification, commitment and rationale for the deliverables or outcome and divides the project into manageable stages, enabling efficient control of resources and regular progress monitoring throughout. The various roles and responsibilities for managing a project are fully described and are adaptable to suit the project's size and complexity, and the skills of the organisation. Project planning using PRINCE2 is product-based which means the project plans are focused on delivering results and are not simply about planning when the various activities on the project will be carried out.

Public Responsibility

The long-term interests of an organisation and its people are best served by adopting an ethical approach and exceeding the expectations and regulations of the community at large.

Q

Quality

The totality of features and characteristics of a product or service which bear on its ability to satisfy stated and implied needs.

Quality Assurance

Confirming the degree of excellence of a product or service, measured against its defined purpose. This might involve a number of techniques. For documentation it might involve inviting informed comment; for software, a process of formal testing, trialling or inviting public feedback on a beta version; for hardware, performance against specified tests; for a management process, comparison with a standard such as BS15000.

Quality Management System

The complete set of quality standards, procedures and responsibilities for an organisation or location.

Queuing Theory

A modelling technique based upon the allocation of requirement to resources. It will indicate whether the resources will meet with the anticipated level and distribution of the demand. Invariably delivered as a computer simulation it provides a prediction of resource requirements, generally mapped against time and business cycles.

Quick Win

Possibly identified by applying the Pareto Principal (cf.) during the initial stages of a Service Improvement Programme (cf.), a Quick Win describes an improvement in actual or perceived service quality, achieved within a short space of time and with relatively little effort. The most significant contribution to a Quick Win is likely to be a common desire to understand the root cause of the lack of service quality and to initiate a corrective Change.

R

RAG (Red Amber Green) Chart
See SLAM Chart.

Real Charging
See *Hard Charging.*

Record
Information in readable form, including computer data, which is created or received and maintained as evidence of performance of an activity. Documents are distinguished from Records by the fact they function as evidence of intentions rather than as evidence of activities. Examples of records include Incident, Problem and Change Records. (cf. *Document*).

Reciprocal Agreement
An IT Service Continuity Planning option that depends on two organisations being willing and able to share their resources, prior to or in the event of an emergency. Capacity and technical compatibility are particular issues.

Recovery
Following failure and repair, the failed Configuration Items (CIs) are recovered into the live infrastructure. This may include recovering data to the last known recoverable state. There may remain further steps before the service is restored to the Users, e.g. testing, transaction re-runs and notifying Users. Recovery is the penultimate stage of the Incident life-cycle.

Recovery Centre
Where an IT unit analyses its full expenditure and investments so that they may be recovered from Customers, usually by formal charging but without profit.

Redundancy
Where a system has been designed to eliminate single points of failure, redundant Configuration Items (CIs) are those which can fail without affecting delivery of the service. However, generally, once a CI has failed, the inherent redundancy will be gone and repair/replacement is required before further failures which would affect the service.

Relationship

Describes the dependency or connectivity between Configuration Items (CIs), using terms such as 'used by', 'part of'', 'connected to', 'resides on'. Relationships not only provide a means of assessing the potential full impact of a proposed Change but can also indicate the potential damage likely to be caused by a single component failure. Relationships are described as 'primary' if they are hierarchical and 'secondary' if not.

Relative Service Priority

In addition to knowledge of activity priorities based upon the given circumstances at a moment in time, services may be awarded a more permanent relative priority, which might be based upon risks to the continuity of important business activities. (cf. *Priority*).

Release

A collection of authorised Changes to an IT service, which are tested and introduced into the live environment together.

Release Acceptance

The process of testing a release, its implementation procedures and back-out plans to obtain a sign-off of its completeness and accuracy.

Release Management

The Service Management process that encompasses the planning, design, build, configuration and testing of hardware and software releases to create a defined set of release components. Release activities also include the planning, preparation, scheduling, training, documentation, distribution and installation of the release to many users and locations. Release Management uses the controlling processes of Change and Configuration Management.

Release Mechanism

The actual equipment, software, techniques or methods used to roll out a release.

Release Plan

A document that describes all of the activities, resources and responsibilities related to a particular release, including the scheduling of that release.

Release Policy
A document that describes the normal roles, responsibilities, release units, normal change content, release frequency and scheduling of releases. The Release Policy is normally part of the Configuration and Change Management Plan.

Release Processes
One of the groups of Service Management processes identified in the BSI Code of Practice, PD0005. Release processes deal with the delivery of new and changed Configuration Items (CIs), hardware, software, documentation, etc. into the live environment.

Release Record
A record containing details of which Configuration Items (CIs) are affected by a release (planned or implemented) and how.

Release Schedule
A document that contains the dates when all releases will be rolled out into the live environment

Release Unit
The portion of the IT infrastructure that is normally released together, for example, a full TP system; a suite; a program; a single module.

Reliability
The ability of a component or IT service to perform a required function under stated conditions for a stated period of time. Reliability is now often taken to include resilience. (cf. *MTBF*).

Remote Fixes
Incidents or Problems resolved without a member of the support staff visiting the physical location in question.

Repair
The replacement or correction of a failed Configuration Item (CI). Repair also refers to the fourth stage of an Incident life-cycle, sitting between Diagnosis and Recovery.

Request for Change

A means of proposing a Change to any component of an IT Infrastructure or any aspect of an IT service. It may be a document or record in which the nature and details of, and the justification and authorisation for the proposed Change are entered.

Request for Service

See *Service Request.*

Resilience

The capability of a set of Configuration Items (CIs) to continue to provide a required function, if not immediately then very quickly, when some CIs in the set have suffered a failure.

Resolution

An action that will resolve an Incident, i.e. allow the users to carry out their business functions. This may be a temporary work-around or the permanent repair or replacement of a faulty CI.

Resolution Processes

One of the Service Management Processes identified in the BSI Code of Practice, PD0005. Resolution Processes (Incident and Problem Management) deal with the concerns of users, identification of Incidents and Problems, their removal and prevention within the infrastructure.

Resource Capacity Management

The Capacity Management task concerned with identifying and understanding the capacity and utilisation of Configuration Items (CIs), ensuring that all finite resources are monitored and measured, and collected data is recorded, analysed and reported; also that the potential use of new technology is tracked and understood.

Responsiveness

Generally, a comparative measurement of the time taken to respond to a particular stimulus. The measurement could be concerned with the speed of an IT system response to a User activity but may equally be used to judge the behaviour of an organisation towards, for example, an Incident or Request for Change.

Restoration of Service

The service is said to be restored when the users are able to process new work i.e. the system and available data have been recovered, appropriate test performed, users informed, and any lost work repeated. Restoration, following Recovery, is the final stage of the Incident life-cycle.

Results Orientation

Balancing and satisfying the needs of all relevant stakeholders (this include the people employed, customers, suppliers and society in general as well a those with a financial interest in the organisation) to achieve excellence.

Return on Investment

The (potential) financial benefit expressed as a percentage of the costs generating that benefit.

Return to Normal

The phase within a business recovery plan which re-establishes norm operations.

Revenue Costs

See *Operational Costs.*

Review

Examination of a completed action, Incident, Change, etc. The purpose of t review is to ensure that completion has been achieved to the satisfaction appropriate stakeholders, identify any lessons learned and feed them into t improvement process.

Risk

A measure of the exposure to which an organisation may be subject. This is combination of the likelihood of a business disruption occurring and t possible loss that may result from such business disruption.

Risk Analysis

Identifying the 'service' value of infrastructure components (assets), t threats to which those assets might be exposed, and the vulnerability of tho assets to the threats identified.

Risk Assessment

Risk Assessment involves analysing risks as a prelude to managing tho risks in order to minimise the effects of unexpected failure.

Risk Management

Management of the risks to assets through the identification, selection and use of countermeasures, justified by the identified risks in terms of their potential impact upon services if failure occurs, and the reduction of those risks to an acceptable level.

Risk Reduction Measure

Measures taken to reduce the likelihood or consequences of a business disruption occurring (as opposed to planning to recover after a disruption).

Role

A set of responsibilities, activities and authorisations.

Roll-out

The activities which deliver, install and commission an integrated set of new or changed Configuration Items (CIs) across logical or physical parts of an organisation.

Roll-out Planning

The process of planning for the physical distribution and deployment of a release into the live environment.

Running Costs

See *Operational Costs.*

Scalability
The measure of a service's ability to increase or decrease in performance an[d]
cost in response to Changes in throughput or demand.

Scaling (of Guidance)
Applying rules, guidance, process, etc. to a size of organisation or proje[ct]
different from its original application. Adapting a process to fit a larger [or]
smaller situation.

Scope
Generally, the extent to which a process or procedure applies. The scope [of]
Configuration Management may not, for example, extend to Custome[r]
information (other than on an 'as informed' basis) and the scope of a Chang[e]
Management procedure may not apply to 'Urgent Changes'. Also a ke[y]
concept in outsourcing, defining which activities are covered by the bas[e]
contract and which are separately chargeable.

Script
See *Diagnostic Script.*

Second Level / Line Support
Technical resources (sometimes based within the Service Desk) called upon b[y]
Incident and Problem Management to assist in the resolution of an Inciden[t,]
restoration of service, the identification of a Problem or Known Error, th[e]
provision of a work-around or the generation of a Change.

Second Line Incident Control
See *'Incident Control Support'.*

Security
The process of ensuring that services are used in an appropriate way by th[e]
appropriate people. In IT Service Management terms, the Confidentiali[ty,]
Integrity and Availability of Configuration Items (CIs) - a task of Availabili[ty]
Management.

Server

A computer on a network that manages resources. Servers are often dedicated, performing no other tasks besides their server tasks, such as the control of files, databases, mail, network traffic, printing or web access.

Service

An integrated composite that consists of a number of components, such as management processes, hardware, software, facilities and people, that provides a capability to satisfy a stated management need or objective.

Service Acceptance Certificate / Document

A certificate or other document that is completed immediately prior to a new or modified service being accepted into the live environment for business use. It provides a degree of confidence that all the required activities have been undertaken to ensure that the service is capable of being delivered to the Customer's satisfaction. Where tasks have not been completed satisfactorily this should be recorded, as should the degree of risk to which these shortcomings are now exposing the business. Based upon that information, the decision can be taken as to whether the new or changed components should be released into the live environment in accord with the current release schedule.

Service Acceptance Criteria

A prioritised list of criteria that a service must meet before the Customer will accept it. They should be defined and agreed with the Customer at the outset.

Service Achievement

The actual service levels delivered by the IT directorate to a Customer within a defined time-span.

Service Capacity Management

A discipline focused on the performance of current services used by the business. It assesses the IT services, their use of resources, working patterns, i.e. peaks and troughs), and ensures that the services can and do meet their Service Level Agreement (SLA) targets.

Service Catalogue

A document (printed or on intranet/internet) produced by the IT department for the information of its Customers and Users. It provides a brief overview, in business terms, of all the business and infrastructure services offered by the IT provider and may include service charges. This information, together with more detailed technical knowledge will be maintained for internal use.

Service Charter
A high level document, endorsed at senior level, which briefly and clearly states the generic standard of service that any Customer or User can expect from the IT department, presented within the context of the Department's IT Service philosophy. It is likely to contain the IT Mission Statement and make reference to the organisation's culture, vision, values and ethical policy.

Service Culture
A Service Culture indicates that, for everyone in the provider organisation, Customer satisfaction is the top priority and that service provider activities demonstrably contribute to the business objectives of the Customer.

Service Definition
See *Service Specification Sheet.*

Service Delivery
Normally, a reference to the five management processes described in the IT Infrastructure Library 'Service Delivery' volume, i.e. Service Level, Capacity, IT Service Continuity and Availability Management, plus Financial Management for IT Services.

Service Design and Management Processes
One of the Service Management Processes identified in the BSI Code of Practice, PD0005. These processes (Availability, Capacity, Continuity, Finance, Security, Service Reporting and Service Level Management) are generally proactive and performed over long time frames. They deal with the effective delivery of appropriate services and service levels to the business Customer.

Service Desk
An alternative name for a Help Desk, often used when the link to other Service Management processes is considered important. It is increasingly the name given to a front line support group who add value by doing a high proportion of first time remote fixes.

Service Hours
The agreed hours when the service is to be available.

Service Improvement Plan / Programme

A formal plan or programme developed when the IT service provider is not currently delivering a service that meets the legitimate Service Level Requirements (SLRs) of the business representative or when greater cost-effectiveness is achievable. The SIP should include clear milestones, which will enable the business representative to judge whether or not timely progress is being made.

Service Level Agreement

A formal negotiated document that defines (or attempts to define) in quantitative (and perhaps qualitative) terms the service being offered to a Customer. Confusion must be avoided over whether the quantitative definitions constitute thresholds for an acceptable service, targets to which the supplier should aspire or expectations that the supplier would strive to exceed. Any metrics included in a Service Level Agreement (SLA) should be capable of being measured on a regular basis and the SLA should record by whom. Typically it will cover: service hours, service availability, Customer support levels, throughputs and responsiveness, restrictions, functionality and the service levels to be provided in a contingency. It may also include information on security, charges and terminology.

Apart from regular periodic reviews, SLAs should be renegotiated whenever a business service is subject to a change of requirement, or there is an inability to deliver to requirement.

Service Level Management

The process of defining, agreeing, documenting and managing levels of Customer service that are required and cost justified. It deals with more than SLAs themselves, including the Service Catalogue and review meetings.

Service Level Objective

A negotiated document that defines the service that will be delivered to a Customer in qualitative terms, although a small number of Key Performance Indicators (KPIs) might also be defined. SLOs are increasingly being preferred, certainly initially, to Service Level Agreements (SLAs) because they provide a clearer understanding of the true nature of the service being offered, focussing on the contribution of the service to the business value chain. Best practice suggests that the business representative should initially draft SLOs.

Service Level Requirement

A document recording the business requirement for an IT service. The SLR belongs to the senior business representative who owns the service. The Service Management Team have a responsibility to support the business representative in drawing up the SLR to ensure that the information contained in the SLR is both comprehensible and comprehensive. The SLR will provide a basis for negotiations linked to the formulation of Service Level Objectives (SLOs) or Service Level Agreements (SLAs).

Service Maintenance Objective

The total time that a component will need to be unavailable to prepare the component for maintenance, carry out maintenance and restore the component to operational use.

Service Management

An element of **Business/IT Alignment** (BITA) (cf.). The high level process that manages IT services on behalf of the business customers. It has authority to make decisions about the delivery of the entire portfolio of IT services. The IT Infrastructure Library (ITIL) sees Service Management as the overall philosophy, which informs the operation of the individual ITIL processes.

Service Management Team

Usually comprising Account Managers, Contract Managers and Service Level Managers. A group of managers who between them provide a coherent approach to the delivery of services. Note that these three roles can, if appropriate to an organisation's structure and resources, be combined in a single role. In some IT departments the SMT also includes Change Management staff.

Service Manager

A senior manager, normally reporting to the IT director, who has overall responsibility for ensuring services are delivered in accordance with agreed business requirements. The Service Manager is also responsible for negotiating requirements with senior business representatives. The Service Manager is responsible for the Service Management Team and is usually a member of the high level Change Advisory Board (CAB). The Service Manager should have a major say in the allocation of resources between services.

Service Outage Analysis
An Availability Management technique used to analyse downtime and to identify opportunities to improve end-to-end service uptime - essentially a Problem Management activity.

Service Owner
The individual taking primary responsibility for a service, including its design, objectives and progression.

Service Planning
Within the major process group of Service Design and Management, Service Planning involves defining service requirements, defining new services, financial planning, defining and modelling service data, defining IT capabilities, benchmarking and gap analysis.

Service Provider
An organisation supplying services or products to customers. The Service Provider may be internal or external.

Service Quality Plan
A plan that underlies the Service Strategy, detailing the internal targets to be achieved within an agreed period, typically one to two years, to improve the agreed service levels and the business perception of service quality.

Service Request
A request for a change, usually both common and straightforward, to be made to a service. A Service Request is characterised by the fact that the Change can be made under strict, well-defined procedural control and is therefore (virtually) risk-free. Providing access to services for a new member of staff and relocating PCs are two typical examples.

Service Specification Sheet
A more detailed definition of a service than is found in the Service Level Agreement (SLA). In effect the Service Specification Sheet contains the information about a service that will constitute the services entry in the Configuration Management Database (CMDB).

Service Strategy

A document agreed between the most senior Customer and IT representatives that lays out future developments in the way that IT resources will be utilised in support of business activities in the long term. A well-formulated Service Strategy will be technology independent.

Service Support

Normally, a reference to the five management processes described in the IT Infrastructure Library 'Service Support' volume, i.e. Incident, Problem, Change, Configuration and Release Management, plus the chapter on the Service Desk function.

Serviceability

The contractual conditions with suppliers covering the availability of, and the conditions under which the contractual conditions are valid for, a Configuration Item (CI) or system.

Severity Code

A simple code assigned to Problems and Known Errors, indicating the seriousness of their effect on the quality of IT service. It is a common name given to the means of recording priority for resolution.

Simulation / Simulation Modelling

Use of a program to simulate computer processing by describing in detail the path of a job or transaction. It can be extremely accurate but requires a great deal of time and effort from the modeller and is therefore very expensive. It is usually only justifiable for business critical systems.

Single Point of Contact

Where all day-to-day communications are channelled through one place. Typically for IT Services this will be the Service Desk. This ensures that Users are able to contact trained staff, all contacts can be recorded consistently, specialist staff are able to concentrate on their work without interruption and work can be co-ordinated and matters dealt with once.

Single Point of Failure

A component that has no back up capability and can cause significant impact to the business if it fails.

Sizing Report

The output of the Application Sizing process. This report indicates the sizing issues for a specific project, including standards for development, monitoring and testing according to the sizing specification.

SLAM Chart

Service Level Agreement Management Chart. This is a grid used to identify at a glance where Service Level Agreements (SLAs) are in danger of being, or have already been, breached. Sometimes coloured red, amber and green to indicate different levels of concern and referred to as a RAG Chart.

SMART Objectives

An objective should comply with principles of it being Simple, Measurable, Achievable, Realistic and Timely.

Society

All those who are, or believe they are, affected by the organisation, other than its people, customers and partners.

Software Environment

Software used to support the application, such as operating system, database management system, development tools, compilers and application software.

Software Process Improvement and Capability dEtermination

Software Process Improvement and Capability dEtermination (SPICE) is a reference process model for software development developed for the International Standards Organisation (ISO). The SEI (cf. *Capability Maturity Model*) was one of the organisations to assist in its development. SPICE is partly based on CMM but, although less specific in determining the elements that must be included for an organisation to reach a certain maturity level, the scope of SPICE is wider than that of CMM and some aspects have been elaborated in more detail.

Specsheet / Specification Sheet

A working document used to specify the customers' requirements (external) and the consequences this has for the service provider (internal), such as required costs, resources and skills and applicable constraints.

Stakeholders

All those who have an interest in an organisation, its activities and its achievements. These may include Customers, partners, employees, shareholders, owners, government and regulators.

Stand-by Arrangements
Arrangements to have available the assets which have been identified as replacements should primary assets be lost following a business disruption. Typically these include accommodation, IT systems and networks and people.

Standard Change
A Change that is recurrent, well known, has been proceduralised to follow a pre-defined, relatively risk-free path, and is the accepted response to a specific requirement or set of circumstances, where authority is effectively given in advance of implementation.

Standard Costs
Pre-determined calculation of expected costs under specified working conditions. Typically used to provide a basis for control through variance accounting, valuation of work, and fixing selling prices.

Standard Operational Task
See *Standard Change.*

Status Accounting
See *Configuration Status Accounting.*

Storage Management
A specific Systems Management activity relating to the policy, techniques and technology deployed to enable the economic and effective storage and maintenance of data.

Strategic
Relating to the highest of the three levels of planning and delivery. Strategic is concerned with the overall goals of an organisation or process.

Structured Systems Analysis and Design Method
Structured Systems Analysis and Design Method (SSADM) is a method used in the analysis and design stages of systems development. Initially developed by the UK *Central Computing and Telecommunications Agency* (cf.) in 1981, SSADM is now a recognised open standard.

Super User
A skilled User (sometimes known as an Expert User) able to deal with first-line support Problems and queries. This is typically in specific application areas, or geographical locations, where there is not the requirement for full-time support staff.

Supply Chain
The delivery of goods, services and information from supplier through to end-User/Customer.

Supply Chain Management
A systematic approach to handling the constituent links in the supply chain.

Support Hours
The hours or times when support, e.g. the Service Desk, is available.

System
An integrated composite that consists of one or more of the processes, hardware, software, facilities and people, that provides a capability to satisfy a stated need or objective.

Systems Management
The tools, policies, procedures and reports used to manage and provide information about an IT infrastructure. Systems Management differs from Service Management in that its focus is on technology rather than process. The key elements of Systems Management include:

- Tools providing for the automation of routine tasks and the reporting of status and event information
- The timely reporting of status information
- The setting of policies for the IT environment such as standardisation, fault tolerance, procurement.

Systems Management has an interface to all Service Management processes, often providing tools and information to support those disciplines.

Systems Outage Analysis
See *Service Outage Analysis.*

Tactical

Concerned with the middle level of planning and delivery. Tactical concerns are around how to achieve an objective (as developed in the strategy) and providing a framework for the operational delivery.

Task

Generically, an activity or set of activities that might be defined as part of a process. When used within a phrase such as 'Standard Operational Task' it defines a well documented, controlled, proceduralised, and usually low risk, activity. The procedure controlling the manner in which the task is carried out would be subject to formal Change Control.

Technical Observation Post

A prearranged meeting of specialist technical support staff from within the IT support organisation brought together to focus on specific aspects of IT availability.

Technical Severity

A simple code assigned to Incidents, Problems and Changes, indicating their underlying technical complexity and their impact on technical resources. Used in conjunction with Business Impact and Business Urgency, it is one of the factors for allocating IT priorities.

Terms of Reference

A document that usually describes the purpose and scope of an activity or requirement.

Test / Test Build Environment

A computer system or discrete part of a computer system (made up of hardware, system software and documentation) which is used to build releases for operational acceptance testing.

Third Line Support

Those supplying support to Second Line teams when they are unable to resolve the issues.

Third Party Supplier

Those external to an enterprise who provide products and/or services that contribute to the overall service provided to Customers.

Threats

The possible causes of disruption that might prevent the delivery of services. Threats act upon the assets of an organisation or a service.

Threshold

A pre-determined level at which action is taken, e.g. the number of occurrences of Incidents attributable to a single Problem or Known Error, the time that an occurrence is outstanding, or the usage levels, at which point some form of escalation procedures are invoked.

Throughput

The volume of work performed on a system or device by the users. Sometimes referred to as 'workload'.

Tied Users

Users who do not have a choice about whether they use the internal IT department's services or not.

Total Cost of Ownership

All the financial consequences of owning an asset. In addition to the initial purchase price this would typically also include maintenance, accommodation charges, opportunity costs, training costs, consumables, internal and external support, interest on capital, etc. (see *Full Cost*)

Total Quality Management

Total Quality Management is a structured system for satisfying internal and external Customers and suppliers by integrating the business environment, continuous improvement and breakthroughs with development, improvement, and maintenance cycles while changing organisational culture.

Transaction Processing

A type of computer processing in which the computer responds immediately to User requests, with each User interaction considered to be a transaction. Automatic teller machines for banks are probably the best-known example.

Transfer Cost

Transfer Costs represent the costs of goods and services 'sold' from one part of an organisation to another, often within a multi-national or other large organisation with a sophisticated internal accounting system. Transfer Costs must be visible in **Cost Models** (cf.) if the true cost of providing services is to be calculated.

Trend Analysis

The process of analysing data to identify underlying longer-term trends, e.g. failure patterns. Used in Incident and Problem Management, it is also employed as a method of modelling in Capacity Management.

Trouble Ticket

A term used in a number of Service Support tools, analogous but not normally directly equivalent to the more precise IT Infrastructure Library terms Incident and Problem.

Tuning

The process of changing the parameters of a device or a system to achieve a specified or improved performance.

U

Unabsorbed Overhead

An indirect cost that cannot be apportioned to a set of Customers and must be apportioned to all Customers in some other manner, such as in proportion to their total absorbed costs, staff numbers, annual budgets, equipment held or work throughput.

Underpinning Contract

A contract with an external supplier covering the delivery of goods and/or services that contribute to the delivery of IT services to Customers. The terms and conditions of underpinning contracts should reflect and be reflected in the appropriate Service Level Agreements (SLAs).

Unit Cost

The cost identified for the use of a single unit of resource consumed or the cost involved in producing a single unit of output, e.g. cost per sheet of paper, per hour of staff time, per invoice generated.

Untied Users

Users who are free to decide whether to obtain IT services from an internal IT department or an external supplier.

Urgency

A measure of business criticality of an Incident, Problem or Change where there is an effect upon business deadlines. The urgency reflects the time available for repair or avoidance before the impact is felt by the business. Together with impact, and perhaps technical severity, it is the major means of assigning priority for dealing with Incidents, Problems or Changes.

Urgent Change

A Change that must be introduced as soon as possible to alleviate or avoid detrimental impact on the business.

Usability

The ease and intuitiveness of a product or service. Low usability will require more support for Users. There are documented and proven approaches to designing, testing and measuring usability.

User / End-User

The people who use the service on a day-to-day basis.

User Forum

Formal meetings of Users of a service or product to identify their views on relevant aspects, including Customer satisfaction, improvements/changes, usability.

V

Value for Money

A concept associated with the economy, effectiveness and efficiency of a service, product or process, i.e. a comparison of the input costs against the value of the outputs and a qualitative and quantitative judgement over the manner in which the resources involved have been utilised and managed. (cf. *Effectiveness, Economy, Efficiency*).

Values

The understandings and expectations that describe how the organisation's people behave and upon which all business relationships are based (e.g. trust, support and truth).

Variable Cost

A cost incurred each time a service is used or a product produced.

Variance

The difference between planned, budgeted or standard cost and actual cost (or revenue). Variance analysis is an analysis of the factors which have caused the difference between the pre-determined standards and the actual results.

Variant

A Configuration Item (CI) that, although different in some small way, has the same basic functionality as other CIs and therefore may be required to be analysed along with its generic group.

Verification

See *Configuration Verification.*

Version

An identified instance of a Configuration Item (CI) within a product breakdown structure or configuration structure for the purpose of tracking and auditing Change history. Also used for software CIs to define a specific identification released in development for drafting, review or modification, test or production.

Version Identifier

A version number, version date or version date and time stamp.

Vision
A statement that describes how the organisation wishes to be in the future.

Vital Business Function
The business critical functions of the business, supported by an IT service.

Voice Over Internet Protocol
Sometimes called 'IP telephony' or 'Voice over the Internet (VOI)', VOIP uses a combination of hardware and software to enable people to use the Internet as the transmission medium for telephone calls.

Vulnerability
A weakness of a service and its constituent Configuration Items (assets) which could be exploited by threats.

Warm Stand-by / Start / Site
See *Intermediate Recovery.*

Waterline

The lowest level of IT detail of relevance to the Customer. Above are the services they use, expressed in their terms. Below it is technical, for IT themselves to deal with.

Wide Area Network

A computer network that spans a relatively large geographical area. Typically, a WAN consists of two or more Local Area Networks (LANs). The largest WAN in existence is the Internet.

Workflow Diagram

A Workflow Diagram (WFD) maps out the way the work is currently done showing each step taken, the decision branches, the time spent, any distances travelled or people contacted, and other important aspects of the work. Having completed the WFD, problem areas can be identified and solutions devised and implemented.

Work in Progress

Tasks formally identified but not yet completed. WIP reports will normally comment on the extent to which WIP is complete and on any aspect of the WIP that changes previous assumptions about time, cost or quality.

Work Instruction

A detailed set of instructions that describe exactly how a low-level activity must be carried out. For example, describing precisely how a Request for Change record is created in the Change Management software support tool. (cf. *Procedure*).

Work-around

A method of avoiding an Incident or Problem, either by employing a temporary fix or technique that means a Customer is not reliant on a Configuration Item (CI) that is known to cause failure.

Workflow Position

The current status or position of an Incident, Problem or Change in its life cycle.

Workloads

Workloads in the context of Capacity Management Modelling, are a set of forecasts which detail the estimated resource usage over agreed planning horizons. Workloads generally represent discrete business applications and can be further sub-divided into types of work (e.g. interactive, timesharing, batch).

Workstation

Although the term is sometimes used to refer simply to a collection of personal desktop devices such as a PC, monitor, printer, etc., it more properly refers to a type of computer used for applications that demand a reasonable amount of computing power and relatively high quality graphics, such as engineering applications, desktop publishing and software development. In terms of computing power, workstations lie between **Personal Computers** (PCs) and **Minicomputers** (cf.). Like PCs, most workstations are single user devices.

Abbreviations and Acronyms

ACD	Automatic Call Distribution
AMDB	Availability Management DataBase
ASP	Application Service Provider
BCM	Business Capacity or Business Continuity Management
BCP	Business Continuity Plan(ning)
BIA	Business Impact Analysis
BITA	Business/IT Alignment
BQF	British Quality Foundation
BRM	Business Relationship Management
BSC	Balanced Scorecard
BSi	British Standards Institution
C&CM	Configuration and Change Management
C&CM Plan	Configuration and Change Management Plan
CAB	Change Advisory Board
CAB/EC	Change Advisory Board / Emergency Committee
CCTA	Central Computer and Telecommunications Agency
CDB	Capacity Management DataBase
CFIA	Component Failure Impact Analysis
CI	Configuration Item
CM	Change/Configuration Management
CMDB	Configuration Management DataBase
CMM	Capability Maturity Model
COP	Code of Practice
CRAMM	CCTA Risk Analysis & Management Method
CRM	Customer Relationship Management
CSF	Critical Success Factor
CTI	Computer Telephony Integration
DBMS	DataBase Management System
DHS	Definitive Hardware Store
DISC	Delivering Information Systems to Customers
DR	Disaster Recovery
DRP	Disaster Recovery Plan(ning)

DSL	Definitive Software Library
EDI	Electronic Data Interchange
EFQM	European Foundation for Quality Management
EXIN	Examen Instituut
FSC	Forward Schedule of Change
FTA	Fault Tree Analysis
GUI	Graphical User Interface
HD	Help Desk
ICT	Information and Communications Technology
ID	Identification
IP	Internet Protocol.
IR	Incident Record/Report
IS	Information System(s)/Information Service(s)
ISEB	Information Systems Examination Board
ISO	International Standards Organisation
IT	Information Technology
ITAMM	IT Availability Metrics Model
ITIL	IT Infrastructure Library
ITSCM	IT Service Continuity Management
ITSM	IT Service Management
*it***SMF**	IT Service Management Forum
IVR	Interactive Voice Response
JD	Job Description
KE	Known Error
KEL	Known Error Log
KER	Known Error Record/Report
KPI	Key Performance Indicator
KSF	Key Success Factors
LAN	Local Area Network
MTBF	Mean Time Between Failures
MTBSI	Mean Time Between System/Service Incidents
MTTF	Mean Time To Fix
MTTR	Mean Time to Repair
OGC	Office of Government Commerce
OLA	Operational Level Agreement
PC	Personal Computer
PER	Project Evaluation Review

PIR	Post Implementation Review
PM	Problem Management
PR	Problem Record/Report
PRINCE2	PRojects IN Controlled Environments
PSA	Projected Service Availability
QA	Quality Assurance
QMS	Quality Management System
RCM	Resource Capacity Management
RFC	Request for Change
RFS	Request for Service (Service Request)
ROI	Return on Investment
SAC/D	Service Acceptance Certificate/Document
SCM	Service Capacity/Supply Chain Management
SIP	Service Improvement Plan/Programme
SLA	Service Level Agreement
SLM	Service Level Management
SLO	Service Level Objective
SLR	Service Level Requirement
SMO	Service Maintenance Objective
SMT	Service Management Team
SOA	Systems Outage Analysis
SPICE	Software Process Improvement Capability dEtermination
SPOF	Single Point Of Failure
SQP	Service Quality Plan
SSADM	Structured Systems Analysis and Design Method
TCO	Total Cost of Ownership
TOP	Technical Observation Post
TOR	Terms of Reference
TP	Transaction Processing
TQM	Total Quality Management
VBF	Vital Business Function
VFM	Value for Money
VOIP	Voice Over Internet Protocol
WAN	Wide Area Network
WFD	Workflow Diagram
WIP	Work in Progress

*it*SMF Ltd.
Webbs Court
8 Holmes Road
Earley
Reading RG6 7BH
United Kingdom
Tel: +44(0)118 926 0888
Fax: +44(0)118 926 3073
e-mail: service@itsmf.com
www.itsmf.com

The itSMF is a totally independent, not-for-profit organisation owned and run by its members. It promotes and helps to set the standards for best practice in IT Service Management. There are national chapters in many parts of the world. For further details of the chapters, and how to contact them, access the web site or contact the UK office.

OGC
Rosebery Court
St Andrews Business Park
Norwich NR7 0HS
United Kingdom
Tel: +44(0)1603 704567
Fax: +44(0)1603 704817
e-mail: info@ogc.gov.uk
www.ccta.gov.uk
www.itil.co.uk

British Standards Institution
389 Chiswick High Road
London W4 4AL
United Kingdom
Tel: +44(0)208 996 9001
Fax: +44(0)208 996 7001
e-mail: info@bsi-global.com
www.bsi-global.com